SAN DIEGO
FIELD INTERROGATION
FINAL REPORT

John E. Boydstun
SYSTEM DEVELOPMENT CORPORATION

PoliceFoundation

The Police Foundation is a privately funded, independent, non-profit organization established by the Ford Foundation in 1970 and dedicated to supporting innovation and improvement in policing. The Foundation's research findings are published as an information service. Conclusions and recommendations are those of the authors and not necessarily those of the Foundation.

PREFACE

The San Diego Police Department Field Interrogation Experiment breaks further ground in the effort to replace hunch and surmise about police practices with empirically derived knowledge. In leading his department to concrete, measured tests of what works in policing, Chief Raymond L. Hoobler has demonstrated the major contributions that can be made by those police departments whose chiefs have the openness of mind to approach critically what they are doing; the resolve to face the hard tasks of scientific experimentation; and the determination to apply the results of experimentation.

The Police Foundation hopes that publication of this report will encourage others to replicate the field interrogation experiment in different kinds of cities. The lessons recorded here from the pioneering San Diego design can help others to plan and implement experiments, perhaps of larger scale, involving larger numbers of beats and police officers, than was feasible in this first field interrogation experiment. The first step points the way.

Patrick V. Murphy
President
Police Foundation

FOREWORD

Our communities look to law enforcement to control crime. With this challenge in mind, law enforcement administrators throughout the United States are currently developing new police strategies and programs designed to control and prevent criminal activity on the street.

However, not only must new programs be developed and tested, but current methods must be studied and evaluated. Ineffective or non-productive activities must be discarded and replaced with new approaches that promise significant results. The efforts of uniformed police officers on the streets of our cities are a key to crime deterrence and prevention as well as to the apprehension of persons involved in criminal misconduct. Their energies must be directed toward activities that effectively deter crime or significantly affect the incidence of crime. Recent studies, sponsored by the Police Foundation, have indicated that random undirected patrol has little deterrent or crime prevention value. Equipped with this information and with the recognition that no longer can the police rely solely on reactive approaches to crime control, police administrators must help develop proactive approaches for utilizing the field officer in the fight against street crime.

A well coordinated field interrogation program, utilizing highly trained officers, is an aggressive, proactive approach to combatting crime where it counts, on the street. Field interrogation programs, however, have, in some communities, become somewhat controversial because of the justifiable concern that these police-citizen contacts could lead to abuse through indiscriminate use. The question of whether a field interrogation program actually has a positive impact on suppressible crime has been of equal concern to police administrators.

In January, 1973, the Police Foundation agreed to sponsor the San Diego Police Department's Field Interrogation Project, a research project designed to examine and evaluate the effectiveness of the Department's field interrogation program. System Development Corporation was selected by the Police Foundation to conduct the evaluation of the project. The conclusions reached during this study are contained in this report, prepared by System Development Corporation's evaluation team; these conclusions, though directly related only to the city of San Diego, should be of value to police administrators in planning or evaluating similar programs.

Our appreciation for their patient and knowledgeable assistance during the study is extended to Richard Staufenberger and Joseph Lewis of the Police Foundation, and John Boydstun and Jack Coale of the System Development Corporation; without their assistance, this project could not have been completed. Acknowlegment is due to the Police Foundation Evaluation Advisory Group for their thoughtful assistance in furthering the analysis of the results. Professors Francine Rabinovitz, Department of Political Science, Massachusetts Institute of Technology; Albert J. Reiss, Jr., Department of Sociology, Yale University; Lee Sechrest, Department of Psychology, University of Florida; and Hans Zeisel, The Law School, University of Chicago, comprise the group.

Raymond L. Hoobler
Chief of Police
San Diego, California

AUTHORS' NOTE

This report presents a summary of the objectives, design, conduct, and evaluation of tests of alternative Field Interrogation Policies. The tests were conducted by the San Diego Police Department under the sponsorship of the Police Foundation. Preparation of this report, conduct of the evaluation, and interpretation of the findings presented herein were the responsibility of System Development Corporation.

The authors are confident that the San Diego project findings are fully supported by the analysis of available data; however, readers are cautioned that the conclusions may not necessarily apply to police departments in other locations, particularly those where Field Interrogation is not a well-established practice.

Evaluation Director	John E. Boydstun
Principal Investigator	Dr. Jack M. Coale
Research Analyst and Statistician	Dr. Zivia S. Wurtele
Field Investigators	Samuel R. McMillen
	Nicholas P. Moelter
	Michael E. Sherry
	Eugene R. Streich

TABLE OF CONTENTS

LIST OF FIGURES

HOW THIS REPORT IS ORGANIZED

In addition to an Executive Summary, this report is organized into six chapters and three appendices. Chapter I presents the background that led the San Diego Police Department to request and receive Police Foundation support for conducting a study of Field Interrogation practices. The chapter also details the specific objectives for the study that ensued.

Chapter II defines the two principal experimental variables that became the framework for the Field Interrogation study project: (1) the suspension of traditional Field Interrogation practices, and (2) the conduct of Field Interrogations by a group of patrol officers who received special training designed to reduce any possible friction between the police and citizen subjects of Field Interrogation contacts.

Chapter III describes the detailed design for evaluating the Field Interrogation study project. Within Chapter III, individual sections delineate how the Systems Development Corporation (SDC) selected control and experimental patrol areas and participating officers, and developed the community survey used to measure public attitudes about police services.

Chapter IV describes the data collection effort including data from the Pre-experimental, Experimental, and Post-experimental periods.

Chapter V presents the results of SDC's analysis of the study. Separate sections address each of the study objectives originally posed in the San Diego Police Department's proposal. Each study question is restated, and findings and conclusions are presented. A summary of the analysis that was performed and details of the analysis are then included.

Chapter VI examines some alternative explanations that might account for the experimental findings presented in this report and identifies areas for further study.

Appendix A contains a listing of the standard curriculum of the San Diego Police Academy. Courses that include material related to Field Interrogations are identified.

Appendix B contains details of the community survey including the actual survey instrument, responses by study area, and the changes that occurred between the pre-experimental and final surveys.

Appendix C contains samples of the Field Interrogation observation logs and observers' reports used by SDC observers of Field Interrogation contacts during the project. Sample copies of completed Field Interrogation reports are also included.

Developing The Supplementary Training Program[5]

On March 2, 1973, the San Diego Police Department sent requests for training proposals to 19 organizations and individuals. The primary objective of the training proposal was to solicit development of an innovative program that would enhance a police officer's ability to conduct an effective Field Interrogation with minimal citizen antagonism. It was also desired that the proposal include the development of a training program that could be utilized in the future for academy training and in-service training, and that the police department's officers actively participate in the development of the program.

In May 1973, after conducting personal interviews with several final contenders, the San Diego Police Department selected Approach Associates to facilitate the training program and to develop a model training curriculum.

The first phase of the training program started on June 25, 1973, with a mass meeting consisting of 25 project officers, consultants from Approach Associates, FI project staff, and chief officers. The second phase in the training process consisted of videotaping and audiotaping the men in the FI role-playing situation. The officers were then able to evaluate themselves (demeanor, safety, approach) while involved in an FI setting. This segment of the training also permitted Approach Associates to gain practical information relating to individual approaches.

In August 1973, the trainees and their supervisors traveled to San Jose, California for the field experiential training phase. The officers were placed in various situations that would attract the attention of the local police. This was an experience that was stimulating and educational. The objective of this phase was to have the officers experience a Field Interrogation from a non-police perspective. Some of the officers felt they were hassled, while others felt they were illegally arrested or physically handled unnecessarily. However, not all of the contact experiences were negative; some very good interrogations were conducted. One of the interesting points of the experience was that the officers in training had to think about what had to be done to attract attention of the local police. This led the trainees to examine their own motives for selecting particular individuals for field interrogation in their own jurisdiction.

The training-workshop program phase was designed to consist largely of informal discussion groups of six to nine officers; sessions were held at the Travelodge Hotel on Harbor Island, from August 7-19, 1973. During these sessions, non-trainees (supervisors) were excluded so that Approach Associates could elicit discussions of the officers' true opinion of the particular subject matter.

Summary Of The Model Training Curriculum[6]

Between June and October 1973, Approach Associates, in conjunction with 25 San Diego patrol officers, developed the model FI training curriculum for the San Diego Police Department. The curriculum is set forth in ten basic units; the units may be presented in different sequences, depending on the seniority of the officers to be trained or the specific training use (see Table 1). To gain maximum impact from this curriculum, it must be implemented as a whole, with modifications for the level of time and seniority within the department. Separate units of the curriculum, however, may be adopted singly or in combination to meet other specific constraints such as time, money, staff, and programs. For example, if legal instruction is adequately provided in the Academy or elsewhere, Unit VI in this curriculum (Legal Aspects of Field Interrogation) could be incorporated in such instruction. Such an approach also applies for Unit IIb (Peacekeeping), Unit III (Safety), and Unit IV (Coping with Cultural Differences). Unit IX (Experiential Training), although extremely valuable, is expensive both in terms of finances (compensation time, transportation, per diem, and so on) and logistics (locating an appropriate jurisdiction, securing the cooperation of the local police department, and protection against adverse consequences to the local department as well as to the sponsoring department). Use of nearby jurisdictions would reduce some of the costs. It should also be noted that the original trainees and the training team considered the experiential training to be one of the most meaningful and unifying components of the training curriculum.

---

[5] Abstracted from a San Diego Police Department staff report.

[6] Abstracted from a report by Approach Associates of Oakland, California.

Table 1
RECOMMENDED COURSE SEQUENCES OF MODEL FIELD INTERROGATION
TRAINING CURRICULUM, FOR USE IN ACADEMY, IN-SERVICE, AND LINE-UP TRAINING

ACADEMY TRAINING SEQUENCE		IN-SERVICE TRAINING SEQUENCE[a]		LINE-UP TRAINING SEQUENCE[b]	
Curriculum Unit	Title	Curriculum Unit	Title	Curriculum Unit	Title
I.	Pre-training preparation: simulated videotaped field contact	I.	Pre-training preparation: simulated videotaped field contact	III.	Safety aspects of Field Interrogation[c]
II.	Police objectives of Field Interrogation: law enforcement and keeping the peace	IX.	Experiential field training	II.	Police objectives of Field Interrogation[d]
III.	Safety aspects of Field Interrogation	VII.	Police environment of Field Interrogation	VI.	Legal aspects of Field Interrogation[e]
IV.	Coping with cultural difference in Field Interrogation	II.	Police objectives of Field Interrogation: law enforcement and keeping the peace	IV.	Coping with cultural difference in Field Interrogation[f]
V.	Techniques for opening and closing a Field Interrogation	III.	Safety aspects of Field Interrogation		
VI.	Legal aspects of Field Interrogation	IV.	Coping with cultural difference in Field Interrogation		
VII.	Police environment of Field Interrogation[g]	VI.	Legal aspects of Field Interrogation		
VIII.	Communications workshops I-A and I-B for Field Interrogation[h]	V.	Techniques for opening and closing a Field Interrogation		
IX.	Experiential field training	VIII.	Communications workshops I-A and I-B for Field Interrogation		
X.	Evaluation	X.	Evaluation		

[a] Recommended for advanced officers, sergeants, or field training officers.
[b] Portions of these units are considered helpful for in-service line-up training.
[c] Especially role-playing selected safety problems.
[d] Especially keeping-the-peace referrals.
[e] Especially new developments in case law.
[f] Especially minority communities' current perceptions of police.
[g] After recruits have spent some time in the field and are about to conclude academy training, this unit should be offered to small groups of 8-10 persons.
[h] After the recruit has completed the probationary period, this unit should be completed with workshops concerned with awareness of impact on FI subject, communication skills, and closing the Field Interrogation.

Videotaping can be a useful adjunct to any training program. It provides one method of dealing with some of the more overt aspects of FI skills. Simulated field contacts, for example, can be taped (curriculum Unit I), and openings and closings (Unit V) can be edited from these tapes and contrasted. A second set of videotapes for use to compare change in FI performance is also instructive. These units are time-consuming, but accommodation for them should be made within the training program, if at all possible.

The minimal FI training curriculum must include at least Unit VIII (Communications Workshops). To fully realize the impact of these workshops on police personnel, however, it is necessary to connect the learning in the workshops to field skills. This, in turn, would require in addition Units IIa (Police Objectives: Law Enforcement) and VII (Police Environment).

An evaluation unit should be included in whatever units or combination of units the department chooses to implement. Evaluation by the participants in any program is essential to future training programs, as well as to present accountability.

Recommended Training

Table 1 shows the different course sequences of the basic ten-unit FI curriculum that are recommended for: (1) academy training of recruits; (2) in-service training of advanced officers, sergeants, or field training officers; and (3) in-service, line-up training. The specific number of units and unit order for each of these three training requirements are presented.

Critique Of The Model Field Interrogation Training Curriculum[7]

The material covered in Approach Associates' curriculum is very similar to material currently being taught in the San Diego Police Academy. Approach Associates covers a variety of topics (legal issues, cultural differences, etc.) under one major heading, Field Interrogations. In the Police Academy, Field Interrogation falls within a category by itself, while legal issues or cultural differences are dealt with specifically through other classes.

The major difference between Approach Associates' curriculum and that of the Police Academy is the former's use of videotaping and field experiential training. Each has its merits and limitations. The limitations of videotaping are the expense of equipment and the need for skilled personnel to operate it. As for field experiential training, due to the large number of recruits attending the Police Academy, the problem of scheduling and actually providing field experiential training would be considerable. Field experiential training requires that officers be taken to an area in which they are not recognized as officers. (This was the purpose of the 25 project officers' traveling to San Jose, California.) The possibility of training 100 or more officers a year, and having them travel to out-of-town locations, is remote; the scheduling and expense involved may outweigh the advantages of field experiential training.

The merits of videotaping include the advantage of officers seeing themselves in action and the opportunity to critique their own (as well as others) performances. They can assess their safety practices, their method of communication, and their general demeanor. The advantage of field experiential training is that it gives officers a feeling of what it is like to be the subject of a Field Interrogation, thereby giving them a broader perspective of community feelings in the context of police functions.

In summary, while the Approach Associates' training and curriculum provide a competent package that addresses many issues, the fact remains that current Police Academy training also addresses the same issues, although perhaps in a different manner and sequence.

---

[7] Abstracted from a San Diego Police Department staff report.

III. THE EVALUATION DESIGN

This chapter presents the evaluation design developed by System Development Corporation (SDC) for evaluating the Field Interrogation (FI) project, along with a detailed discussion of the approach used to arrive at the selected design. The activities comprised selecting Control, Special FI, and No-FI Areas; selecting officers to participate in the study; and selecting households to participate in the community survey.

OVERVIEW OF THE EVALUATION DESIGN

SDC's design required the selection of three study areas (one for control and two for experimental conditions) that were closely matched in terms of their demographic and socioeconomic compositions and in their prior reported crime histories.

In the *Control Area*, Field Interrogations were to be conducted with no changes from normally practiced activities. In the *Special FI Area*, Field Interrogations were to be conducted only by officers who were to be given special supplemental training in the conduct of Field Interrogations by Approach Associates. In the *No-FI Area*, Field Interrogations were to be suspended for a nine-month Experimental period.

Community attitude surveys were to be conducted in each of the areas both prior to and following the nine-month experimental period. Additionally, a variety of information was to be collected for analysis. Data were to be collected for three time periods—Pre-experimental, Experimental, and Post-experimental:

- Crime history data on crimes considered to be suppressible by patrol
- FI-history data
- Arrest-history data
- Complaint-history data
- Sampling of report details from arrests made by Control and Special FI officers
- Observation reports of FI encounters
- Race/ethnicity and age characteristics of FI subjects
- Sample of reasons-for-stop for Field Interrogations
- Use of FI information by investigators.

The focus of the SDC analysis was threefold: first, to determine the statistically significant *changes* that occurred *within* each of the three areas between the Pre-experimental (baseline) period, the Experimental period, and the Post-experimental period; second, to identify the *differences in changes* that occurred *among* the three areas (that is, the rates and directions of changes in the three areas were to be compared), and third, to interpret the findings in terms of their relationship to the three alternative FI practices being tested.

SELECTION OF AREAS

SDC's selection of experimental areas was guided by three major considerations:

- The areas should be representative of typical areas in the city and should be closely matched in terms of their demographic, socioeconomic, physical, and crime history characteristics.

- To facilitate the maintenance of experimental controls and project supervision, the areas should all be in the same patrol district.
- Because of operational considerations and financial limitations, each area should be limited in size to a single patrol beat.

Since the planned analysis was to focus on the relative changes occurring within the selected areas, total area populations and geographical sizes were not controlling considerations.

Approach

The city of San Diego is divided into three major police patrol districts—northern, central, and southern. Each district is further divided into supervisor areas, and finally into patrol beats. Each beat is composed of a grouping of contiguous census tracts.

The San Diego Police Department maintains reported crime statistics by census tract as well as by patrol beat. Periodically, the size of patrol beats is adjusted by adding or subtracting census tracts. Such adjustments are done to provide a more equitable balance of the patrol workload among the beats within each patrol district. The coincidence between census boundaries and patrol beat boundaries makes it relatively easy to compare the demographic and socioeconomic characteristics of patrol beats or larger areas.

Because of dissimilarities between operations and the incidence of crime among the three administrative districts (northern, central and southern), it was tentatively decided that all study beats should be within the same administrative district. This decision also facilitated the control of the experiment, since all involved personnel would be operating under the same administrative control.

A secondary decision to select beats within the central administrative district was taken for three additional reasons: (1) Patrol operations in the large rural areas of the northern and southern administrative districts are dissimilar in many ways from the central district and are thus not representative of the rest of San Diego and do not share the characteristics of most other US cities of similar size and population. Together they constitute less than 24 percent of the city population. (2) The northern district is almost completely White (averaging 90 percent or more, per beat) while the southern district is far above the mean city distribution to Spanish-speaking population (averaging over 30 percent, as against the city mean of 12.6 percent). (3) These administrative districts are separated geographically from the central district.

SDC's objective in the selection of candidates for the experiment was to identify areas that are representative of San Diego, but that deviated moderately in their proportion of White (non-Spanish) residents and in their proportion of youth. The primary selection criterion was that the beat have a greater than average minority population and also a significant White population. The second criterion to be satisfied was that the beat be at least representative of the city in its proportion of youth. The third criterion was that the beat be representative of the city in demographic, socioeconomic, physical, and crime characteristics.

Since beats were designed (by combining contiguous census tracts) so as to equalize crime rates, the task was reduced to that of developing a methodology for comparing beats on the basis of the first three of these characteristics. The source of this information was the 1970 Census of Population and Housing. The data were obtained from three different census summary tape releases, based upon 100, 20 and 15 percent sample survey data.

For each of the 90 beats, the values of 26 variables were computed. These variables are listed in Table 2. It may be noted that 13 of the variables fall in the first grouping (demographic), seven in the second grouping (socioeconomic), and six in the third grouping (physical neighborhood). The number of variables assigned to each of these categories influenced SDC results in scoring the beats with respect to their deviations from the San Diego beat average. These numbers assumed the role of weights and reflected the relative importance that SDC attributed to the three categories for the purposes of this study. This type of decision was obviously subjective, but was founded on the experience SDC has had in evaluating the importance of these variables in relation to crime rates. SDC assigned a weight to the demographic group that equaled the sum of the weights for the other two groups. This decision reflected, in part, the significance of sex, age, and race/ethnicity differences in reported contacts with police.

A measure of the deviation, or distance, of a beat from the average for the 90 San Diego beats was derived as follows. Each variable was transformed to a standardized Z score. A Z score is simply the number of standard deviations that a beat's value for a given variable is from the mean value of that

Table 2
SAN DIEGO POLICE DEPARTMENT BEAT COMPARISONS

CENSUS CHARACTERISTICS	CONTROL (BEAT 22)	NO-FI (BEAT 26)	SPECIAL FI (BEAT 28)	TOTAL CITY
Population[a]	8,725	14,629	7,412	701,654
Male (%)	48.4	48.9	48.9	51.3
Female (%)	51.6	51.1	51.1	48.7
Age Distribution (%)				
0 - 5	11.3	15.3	14.5	9.7
6 - 12	14.7	22.0	21.5	11.7
13 - 15	5.8	6.9	7.3	4.5
16 - 19	6.1	5.7	6.3	7.1
20 - 34	20.1	21.3	20.8	25.6
35 - 49	18.2	18.5	18.0	16.7
50 & over	23.8	10.3	11.4	24.7
Race/ethnicity distribution (%)				
White[b]	67.6	68.2	69.7	69.8
Spanish-American	12.2	19.6	22.1	16.4
Black	17.5	5.7	4.8	9.4
Other	2.7	6.5	3.4	4.4
Families				
Female head (%)	11.4	12.8	12.1	14.8
Below poverty (%)	8.2	11.0	8.2	11.8
Average size	3.4	4.1	4.1	3.3
Median income ($)	10019.	9441.6	9946.	9438.
Education (median years)	12.2	12.2	12.2	12.2
Housing units				
Single (%)	84.7	73.9	97.1	57.5
1 - 10 (%)	8.2	8.7	3.3	20.9
Over 10 (%)	0.2	17.2	0.0	18.6
Mobile units (%)	6.9	0.0	0.0	3.2
Non-standard (%)	1.0	2.2	0.4	6.6
Overcrowded (%)	1.6	2.8	3.1	2.9
Median value ($)	18094.9	19594.1	17907.1	21470.
Median rent ($)	110.3	115.1	125.9	114.
Sum of Z scores ΣZ^z	5.62	10.37	13.78	—

[a]Population was not a variable in the computation of Z scores.
[b]White excludes Spanish-Americans.
 Source: Based on 1970 Census data.

variable for all beats. A Z score is computed by subtracting the mean value from the beat's value and dividing the resultant difference by the standard deviation. The sum of the squares of all 26 Z scores for a beat was then used as a measure of that beat's total distance (or variation) from the average beat. This measure is subjective, depending upon judgment for the choice of variables employed to describe the beat. However, once this choice is made, this technique for measuring the deviation of a beat from the average for the 90 San Diego beats provides a reasonable procedure for identifying these beats that are representative of the city.

16

The first step in the search for beats that satisfy the requirements of this study was to identify those beats in the central district that were at or below the beat-average percent White (non-Spanish) but that contained at least 35 percent White (non-Spanish) population. Fifteen beats satisfied this condition.

The second step was to introduce the youth criterion. This resulted in the elimination of four beats that were below the city beat-average in percent of population in the two teenage categories (13-15 years and 16-19 years). The remaining beats, together with their Z score measures of distance from the average for the 90 San Diego beats were as follows:

BEAT	Z SCORE MEASURE OF DISTANCE FROM SAN DIEGO BEAT AVERAGE
4	124.12
8	28.91
9	48.59
11	22.73
12	15.79
16	9.59
22	5.62
26	10.37
27	16.83
28	13.78
29	10.76

Of the 90 San Diego beats, more than half (46) have Z score distances from the average that are greater than 16.83. On the basis of the third criterion—being representative of the city of San Diego—beats were eliminated that scored higher than 16.83. Beats 12, 16, 22, 26, 27, 28, and 29 remained.

A fourth criterion related to control was to select beats under the same line supervision, if possible. Beats 22, 26, 27, 28, and 29 were within supervisory district 754. Applying this criterion to district 754, beats 12 and 16 were eliminated. There were additional reasons for elimination of these beats: from the perspective of experimental control, they are so located as to experience an excessive amount of police vehicle traffic as the units go to and from their beats, headquarters, and jail facilities.

To aid in the choice of a final three beats from the five remaining, discussion was initiated with Chief Hoobler, several assistant chiefs, Inspector Reierson, and the project staff. Operational considerations and the amenability of these beats to rigid experimental controls were closely examined. In order to avoid possible spill-over effects, it was decided that no two of the study areas should be contiguous. Maximum isolation of the Special FI and No-FI beats from the Control beat and from all other beats where traditional FI practices would continue also appeared desirable. These considerations resulted in the selection of beat 22 as the Control area, beat 28 as the Special FI Area, and beat 26 as the No-FI Area. Table 2 displays census data for the three areas and Figure 1 is a map that displays the boundaries of the central station beats, and further indicates those beats selected for the experiment. All beats in the 100-series are under the administration of the northern station. Southern station beats (90-series) are off the southern edge of the map, beyond National City and Chula Vista.

The area immediately to the north and east of beat 28 and to the south and east of beat 26 is unincorporated and thus is under the law enforcement jurisdiction of the Sheriff of San Diego County. This area is a developed, largely residential, area that closely resembles that of beats 28 and 26.

The area to the west and northwest of beat 26 is incorporated as National City, which has its own police department. Those areas of National City immediately adjacent to beat 26 closely resemble the residential developments in beat 26.

To protect the integrity of these study areas, the following wording was inserted into the approved evaluation plan:

Although the SDPD normal research and planning procedures allow the adjustment of beat boundaries on relatively short notice to accommodate seasonal changes and other anomalies of crime and calls-for-service shifts, the beats selected for the FI experiment will retain their integrity throughout the experiment.

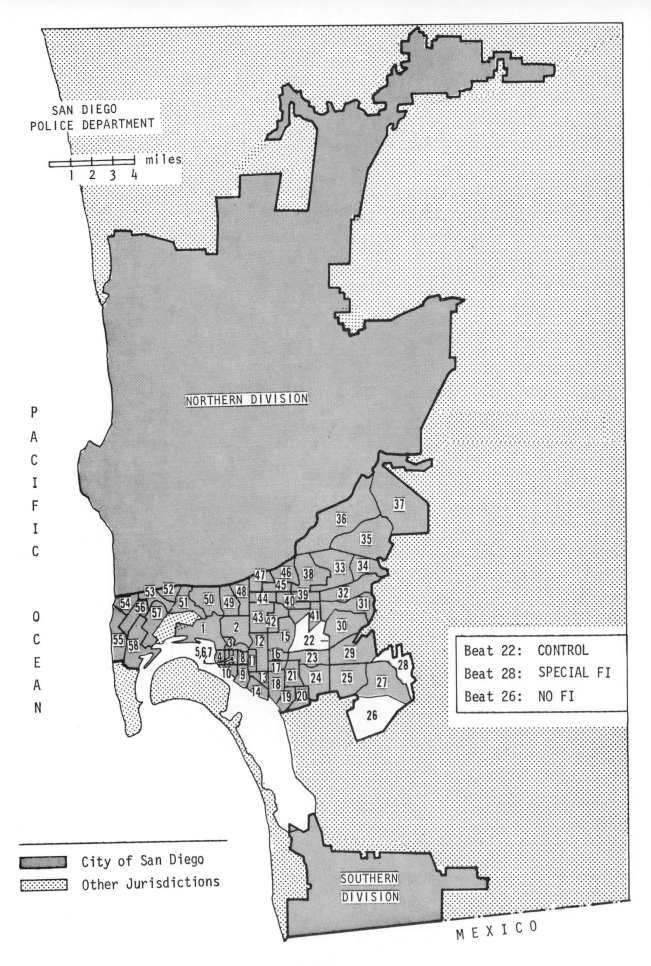

San Diego Police Department

miles
1 2 3 4

PACIFIC OCEAN

NORTHERN DIVISION

Beat 22: CONTROL
Beat 28: SPECIAL FI
Beat 26: NO FI

SOUTHERN DIVISION

MEXICO

City of San Diego
Other Jurisdictions

Figure 1
FIELD INTERROGATION STUDY AREA MAP

Unfortunately, one month after the Experimental period of the FI study began, the police department found it necessary to redraw the boundaries and renumber all patrol beats in the city. This re-configuration was not motivated by changes in the study area, but as a result, the three selected areas lost their identity as individual patrol beats. There were, however, no changes in the planned patrol operations or in the levels of patrol activity within the selected areas because experimental controls were maintained by the San Diego Police Department's project coordinator and were monitored by SDC to ensure that: (1) no Field Interrogations were conducted in the No-FI Area; (2) *only* the specially trained patrol officers would conduct Field Interrogations in the Special FI Area; and (3) *only* patrol officers without special FI training would conduct Field Interrogations in the Control Area.

The major study complication resulting from the beat re-configuration was that report statistics had to be manually compiled by the project staff for the study areas, rather than using the convenient beat tabulations that are computer-generated by the department. Fortunately, the department maintains crime statistics on a census tract basis as well as by beat so that the study area tabulation process was not overly difficult. Special arrangements were made to ensure accurate and complete reporting of all Field Interrogations and arrests made in the study areas. Other report data, however, were more difficult to tabulate. For example, details of arrests for one study area could be tabulated only by manually comparing officer reports with duty rosters and with address guides for the study areas. This situation created additional work but did not compromise the objectives of the evaluation effort.

SELECTION OF OFFICERS

Officers selected to participate in the special training course in FI methods and procedures and in the subsequent experiment were those who were already assigned to the Experiment beat and its contiguous beats. Assignment of officers to these beats had been made prior to the selection of the beats for the experiment and therefore was not expected to bias the results. The officers serving contiguous beats were included in the training to provide a buffer of experimentally trained patrol officers around the actual Special FI Area. (The wisdom of this decision became apparent when the beat re-configuration took place.)

Those officers who were assigned to the selected No-FI Area were also to be given the special FI training. This decision was based on the assumption that the training would help them understand the experiment and thus be more willing to adhere to the FI moratorium.

A total of 25 officers were selected for training. Some screening was necessary to determine officer willingness and availability to serve on the selected beats for the duration of the project. A few who could not project the required time on the beat for various reasons (such as being due for promotion or for transfer to another section of the city) were transferred prior to the beginning of the training and replaced by persons with a reasonable projection of longevity on the selected beats. Replacements were selected from those officers who had previously requested assignment to the selected areas.

These procedures were used to minimize the bias that could have been introduced by selecting volunteers for the program. No special controls were placed on those officers assigned to the Control Area other than that they would not receive the special FI training.

THE COMMUNITY SURVEY

Objectives

The use of a community survey was designed to measure community attitudes toward crime or police operations that might be influenced by the FI experiment. A secondary objective was to attempt to identify any subgroups of the general population that could be associated with a particular set of attitudes.

Because the objective was to measure changes in public attitudes that might be associated with alternative FI practices, the decision was made to withhold any public announcement or publicity about the experiment.

The survey instrument included nine respondent measures:
- Demographic and socioeconomic characteristics
- Personal acquaintance with police
- Fear of crime and crime probability in the neighborhood

- Experience with crime (as victim or witness)
- Experience with police-initiated contacts
- Opinions about local crime trends and causes
- Opinions about police patrol operations
- Opinions about police rights in FI situations
- Satisfaction with responses to calls for service.

Survey Instrument

Development of the San Diego community attitude survey was based on the questionnaire used for the Kansas City Preventive Patrol Experiment. The survey instrument provided by the Police Foundation was modified by SDC in consultation with Mr. Tony Pate of the Kansas City Police Foundation Evaluation Staff and with Dr. Oscar Kaplan, the survey contractor.

The original instrument could not be used, first, because of funding and time constraints. The survey contractor and SDC determined that 30 minutes was the maximum allowable time for questionnaire administration; consequently, it was necessary to reduce the Kansas City questionnaire administration time by more than 50 percent.

Second, the San Diego population target groups were expected to differ from those in Kansas City in having a high proportion of persons of low educational status and persons whose primary language is Spanish. Consequently, the structure of the Kansas City questionnaire was modified to make it more comprehensible to the San Diego target communities.

Third, the San Diego study focuses on police-community relations with regard to a single patrol function—Field Interrogations—while the Kansas City study was more broadly directed. Consequently, the Kansas City instrument was tailored by SDC to meet the needs of the San Diego study.

Although numerous changes were made, some comparability remained between the San Diego and Kansas City questionnaires. It should be possible to compare results on the items that remained substantially the same.

Community Survey Sample

The same sampling design was employed for both the 1973 pre-experiment and the 1974 post-experiment surveys. Approximately equal samples were drawn from each of the three study areas. In each area, a probability sample of occupied housing units was drawn so that each household had an equal probability of being included in the sample. For any included household, each member 16 years or older had an equal chance of being chosen as respondent. The sample in each area was a replicated sample, composed of two independent sample-halves. Sampling involved two stages—the selection of clusters of six adjacent housing units and the selection of the respondent to be interviewed in each household. Clusters of housing units for the second survey were adjacent to those of the first survey. No household was interviewed twice.

The sample design was rigid in that it did not permit the interviewers any freedom in the selection of either the housing units or the respondent. No substitution was permitted for an intended respondent who could not be reached after three call-backs or who refused to be interviewed. These restrictions were necessary in order to maintain the scientific basis for making inferences about the population based on the sample.

The response rate (measured as percent of occupied housing units in the sample for which interviews were completed) was 74 percent for the first survey and 78 percent for the second. The corresponding numbers of completed interviews were 541 and 607, respectively.

Demographic differences between respondents and those who refused to participate were similar for the two surveys. In each survey, those who refused to respond included a larger proportion of females, of older people, and of home (rather than apartment) dwellers. In the case of the first survey, the group that refused to participate also included a slightly larger proportion of Whites. Details are available in the Appendix B to this report (see Tables B-1, B-2, B-3 and B-4).

As a check on the sampling procedures and on whether socioeconomic or demographic changes had occurred in any of the three areas during the year of the experiment, responses to the second part of the questionnaire were compared for the two surveys. Frequencies of response to each question in the two surveys were compared separately for each area. Chi-square tests of significance of differences in response between the surveys were computed.

Based upon this analysis, it was concluded that, within each area, the samples of the two surveys were quite similar in socioeconomic and demographic composition. In no area were changes in response significant for number of children, owner/renter, age, education, marital status, principal wage earner, sex, and ethnic background.

In very few cases, results were significantly different at the .05 level. In the case of occupation, differences were significant in the Control Area, but not in either of the other areas. In the Control Area, there was a slight decline in professionals and managers and an increase in clerical and service occupations. No major pattern of change in occupational status was detected.

Income increased significantly in the Special FI Area, but did not change significantly in either of the other areas. People's source of news changed significantly in the Control Area (less reliance on newspapers), but not in other areas.

The interviewers' evaluations of housing units, compared with others in the neighborhood, did not change significantly in the Control Area, but did change significantly in each of the other areas: the percentage of houses in the *average* category increased in the No-FI Area, while there was a significant percentage shift from *average* to *above-average* in the Special FI Area.

In summary, all indications are that the samples are valid representations of the citizens of the study areas and, to a lesser extent, of all of the citizens of San Diego.

CRIME STATISTICS

The monthly crime statistics used in this analysis pertain to crime types that, first, are reported by citizens and second, that are considered by San Diego Police Department to be suppressible crimes, that is, crimes that can potentially be reduced through police actions. The only crime statistics maintained by patrol beat and month by the San Diego Police Department are on suppressible crimes.

San Diego's suppressible crimes list includes six of the seven Part I-crimes, as defined in the FBI's *Uniform Crime Reporting Handbook* (July 1966). San Diego excludes the seventh, criminal homicide, but adds two crime types: sex offenses and malicious mischief/disturbances. The relationship between the *Uniform Crime Reporting* (UCR) Part I Crime Definitions and San Diego's suppressible crimes is shown in Table 3.

Table 3
A COMPARISON OF FBI UCR CRIME CATEGORIES WITH
SAN DIEGO POLICE DEPARTMENT'S SUPPRESSIBLE CRIMES

UCR PART I—CRIMES	SAN DIEGO POLICE DEPARTMENT'S SUPPRESSIBLE CRIMES
Criminal homicide	Excluded
Forcible rape	Reported with sex offenses[a] as sex crimes
Robbery	Same
Assault	Same
Burglary	Same
Larceny/theft	Same, but reported in two categories as grand theft and petty theft
Auto theft	Same
UCR total Part I crimes	Total suppressible Part I crimes + Malicious mischief/disturbances[b] Total suppressible crimes

[a]San Diego's reported sex crimes includes UCR Part I forcible rapes, plus UCR Part II sex offenses.
[b]San Diego's malicious mischief/disturbances is the equivalent of UCR's Part II categories of vandalism and disorderly conduct.

DATA TO BE COLLECTED

A variety of Pre-experimental, Experimental, and Post-experimental time period data were to be collected for analysis. Nine specific types of data were to be collected:

- Monthly counts of suppressible crimes, by type, for each of the areas
- Monthly counts of Field Interrogations for each of the areas
- Monthly counts of total arrests, by area
- History of complaints against the department generally and complaints from the study areas, with special reference to FI-generated complaints
- Observation reports of FI encounters witnessed by trained observers
- Details of FI reports during the Experimental period including race/ethnicity, and age characteristics of FI subjects in each area, and the officer's suspicion about the subject's crime potential
- A one-month sample of the details of arrests made by officers assigned to the study areas, with regard to the precipitating cause for arrest, the formal charges, the age, race/ethnicity, and residence of subjects, and the resulting case disposition
- The use of and attitudes toward FI information, as reported by a survey of investigators
- Frequency of requests by investigators or others to examine FI source documents.

IV. DATA COLLECTION

This chapter presents a discussion of the types of data collected to establish a baseline, and the types of data collected during and following the actual study. Baseline data were collected on crime statistics, calls for service, and citizen complaints. The community survey conducted in August 1973 also became a portion of the baseline. Experimental time period data were collected from crime reports, FI reports, arrest reports, observations of officers conducting Field Interrogations, and interviews with FI subjects. Data collected in the Post-experimental period were from crime reports, arrest reports, and FI reports.

BASELINE DATA

Statistics, by beat, for suppressible crimes were available spanning the seven-month interval between the last beat re-configuration, February 1973, and the start of the FI experiment in August 1973. Only four months of beat arrest data (May through August of 1973) were available, due to a change in the manual tabulation process of counting arrests. Prior to May, juvenile arrests were not included in the tabulation.

Because of the department's procedures for filing and handling FI reports at the time, it was not possible to establish a Pre-experimental baseline of Field Interrogations generated in the study areas. The monthly tabulation of Field Interrogations then in use by the department was taken from officers' daily reports and not from an actual count of FI reports submitted. Officers routinely conduct Field Interrogations in beats other than their own. A special manually tabulated sample by area was accomplished for the one-month period, April 8 through May 8, 1973.

Partially because of this sampling problem (and prior to the start of the FI experiment), the department instituted a departmentwide change in FI report forms and handling procedures. Among other things, the changes provided for actual counts of FI reports by beat. Because of the small baseline sample size and the changes in reporting procedures, System Development Corporation (SDC) could not draw any conclusions as to the overall effects of the FI experiment on the number of FI reports written.

A search of available departmental citizen complaint records revealed that records by beat were not available for the full seven-month baseline period. However, a special tabulation had been previously performed for the period between April 1 and June 30, 1973. During that quarter, a total of 574 complaints had been received by the department, 52 (9.0 percent) of which had resulted from Field Interrogations. None of the 52 had occurred in any of the study areas. Provision was made to keep complaint records by beat during the Experimental period.

SDC's analysis of the first community survey, conducted by August 1973 by Economic Behavior Analysts under a separate contract from the Police Foundation, also became a portion of the baseline data.

EXPERIMENTAL PERIOD DATA

Field Interrogation Reports

The department instituted new FI reporting forms and processing procedures prior to the start of the Experimental period. The revisions temporarily made it easy for SDC to collect accurate and detailed information about those Field Interrogations written in the Control and Special FI Areas during the experiment. Unfortunately, the beat re-configuration that occurred one month into the study largely negated the advantages of the reporting improvements and necessitated manual tabulations. The manual process, although cumbersome, is believed to have resulted in accurate counts of all Field Interrogations performed in the study areas.

Arrest Reports

Accurate manual counts were kept by the department of total arrests made in the three study areas. As a method of accounting for FI contacts that resulted in on-the-spot arrests by the patrol officers, all arrest report forms and juvenile contact report forms were overprinted with a series of boxes to be checked by the arresting officer to indicate the event (reason-for-stop) resulting in the arrest. Category options were: Field Interrogation, traffic stop, radio dispatch, warrant, and other. These modified forms were in the field by December 1973 and arrangements were made by the project coordinator with the records and juvenile divisions to keep a monthly departmentwide tally of arrests, by reason-for-stops, prior to filing the arrest forms in the suspects' packets.

To determine any differences between the quality of arrests and the characteristics of subjects arrested by officers assigned to the study areas, a one-month sample (March 1974) of the details of arrest reports for officers working these areas was examined. The procedure for gaining access to arrest details was somewhat complicated in that it necessitated: (1) manually extracting the names of those arrested from the individual daily activity reports of each of the study officers; (2) going with this list of names to the records section, and pulling the individual suspect files; (3) determining the precipitating cause of the arrest and subject characteristics; and (4) from a separate document, ascertaining the disposition of the case.

Determination of arrest dispositions was made only to the extent that an arrest was rejected or filed (adults held-to-answer by the district or city attorney, and juveniles referred to juvenile hall or probation). Court findings were considered to be beyond the purview of this study.

Ride-Along Observations

To assess the possible differences between trained and untrained officers' behavior, and to give insight into the community relations effects generated by officer behavior, a schedule of ride-along observations of both Control and Experimentally trained officers was conducted.

Recognizing the wide range of variables in the types and extent of patrol activities that might be related to such factors as day of week, hour of day, or season of year, and to the requirement to observe the behavior of as many Special FI officers as possible and at least a like number of Control officers, a rather elaborate sampling schedule of ride-along observations was formulated. All observations were conducted by the same four SDC evaluators, each of whom had extensive patrol observation experience prior to this project.

Initially it was intended that one observer would ride with the officer(s) under scrutiny, while a second observer would ride in a follow-car to conduct post-FI interviews with FI subjects and with witnesses. This plan was not implemented because of some difficulties in scheduling the necessary reserve officers to drive or accompany the second observer. As the observers gained experience it also became apparent that too few Field Interrogations take place on any given shift to warrant the expense of the follow-car (the average proved to be less than one Field Interrogation per beat, per watch). Moreover, very few witnesses to FI situations were encountered. In only four instances during the observations for the October through December quarter were witnesses or bystanders present, and in each case, these were juveniles. Several factors contribute to this fact. In the event of car stops, since all occupants of the car are usually interrogated—at least to the extent of being asked to identify themselves—they become subjects rather than witnesses. Many, if not most, pedestrian contacts are initiated because individuals are observed alone or in pairs at unusual places and times and thus all present are subjects of questioning. Finally, since any given officer on any shift may have few occasions to interrogate, project manpower could better be distributed to observe more officers.

A great deal of project manpower, time, and money was expended on observations during the period September 1973 through February 1974. By February it was apparent to all four observers that many hours of observation resulted in relatively few observations of Field Interrogations. It was also deemed inappropriate to suggest that more interrogations be conducted by officers under observation.

Supervisors of patrol officers continually reminded patrol officers to conduct their beat activities as though there was no one observing their activities.

Typically, most patrol officers initiating a Field Interrogation think "this looks like a possible Field Interrogation." The officers then proceed with both close observation and interrogation, entering relevant information in notebooks. At some point during the process the officers either confirm or reject their original hunch. If they consider that the situation meets the criteria for a Field Interrogation, they can then complete the FI form, using their notes and immediate memory for descriptive data.

It is not always clear to an observer, or to the patrol officer, when a Field Interrogation is either about to occur or is in progress. To a considerable extent, the decision to field interrogate is an emergent event arising out of a particular set of circumstances. For example, what may start out as a routine traffic stop for an inoperative taillight may end up as a full-fledged Field Interrogation, due to information cues provided by initial questioning and observation. On the other hand, an officer planning to stop and Field Interrogate a suspicious-looking loiterer may, upon discovering that the person has legitimate reasons for being at that location, disregard (not complete) the Field Interrogation.

In either instance the observer may not be entirely certain of what situational cues the officer is operating under during the course of an on-scene officer-citizen interaction, or indeed, whether or not a Field Interrogation has occurred until after the fact.

In all, approximately 625 hours of observation during 96 shifts were conducted to observe 42 Field Interrogations by Special FI officers and 37 Field Interrogations by Control officers. The total number of individual officers observed was 23 Special FI officers, including two sergeants, and 38 Control officers, including two sergeants. A sample observer's log and two FI observation forms are included in Appendix C.

In January 1974, it was recommended to the Foundation that ride-along observations be curtailed in favor of increased emphasis by evaluation personnel on two other matters: (1) the close scrutiny of daily activity report summaries of officers departmentwide to determine the relationships between field contacts and FI slips submitted, and between arrests and Field Interrogations, and (2) a study of investigators' use or non-use of Field Interrogations, and their reported reasons.

Observer Interviews Of Field Interrogation Subjects

During the course of the ride-along observations, 42 attempts were made by the observers to interview the subjects of Field Interrogations. In most cases it was not appropriate to attempt to interview the subjects at the scene of the Field Interrogation. Either further delay of the subject would affect the subject's attitude toward the initial stop, or the situation was such that the officer with whom the observer was riding had pressing business elsewhere (such as a radio call or traffic enforcement requirement).

Nine subjects were interviewed by observers on the street immediately following the Field Interrogation by the officer. Nineteen subjects were contacted by telephone subsequent to their interrogation. Attempts were made to contact 14 other individuals, but because of incorrect telephone numbers or addresses, refusal to talk with an interviewer, or because they were untraceable military personnel, no contact was possible.

Other Data Sources

In addition to the data elements enumerated above, other data sources were examined and recorded for application to the investigation. These sources and uses included, first, actual counts of suppressible crime reports, by crime type and study area, and second, a survey of all investigators working out of the central division to ascertain their use of Field Interrogations and their views of FI reports as an investigative tool.

POST-EXPERIMENTAL PERIOD DATA

The second community attitude survey was conducted in the study areas, and five months of data were collected after the conclusion of the field experiment, that is, after Field Interrogations were resumed in the No-FI Area. Three types of data were amassed:
- Counts of crime reports of suppressible crimes, by type and by study area
- Arrest reports-total counts, by study area only (no arrest details)

• FI reports-total counts, by study area only (no FI details).

Although not planned in the original evaluation design, the collection and the analysis of these data were incorporated into the evaluation to provide further insights into the effects of alternative FI practices.

Table 4 summarizes, for the three study periods, the availability (by number of months) of eleven categories of data used in the evaluation.

Table 4
SUMMARY OF DATA AVAILABILITY BY STUDY PERIOD

DATA CATEGORY	PRE-EXPERIMENTAL PERIOD Feb. '73-Aug. '73	EXPERIMENTAL PERIOD Sept. '73-May '74	POST-EXPERIMENTAL PERIOD June '74-Oct. '74
Monthly counts of crime reports (suppressible crimes by type and beat)	Feb. '73-Aug. '73 (7 months)	Sept. '73-May '74 (9 months)	June '74-Oct. '74 (5 months)
Counts of FI Reports by beat	Apr. '73	Sept. '73-May '74 (9 months)	June '74-Oct. '74 (5 months)
Details of FI Reports	None	Sept. '73-May '74 (9 months)	None
Counts of total arrest by beat	May '73-Aug. '73 (4 months)	Sept. '73-May '74 (9 months)	June '74-Oct. '74 (5 months)
Arrest: reasons-for-stops	None	Dec. '73-May '74 (6 months)	None
Arrest details: subject's age, race, residence, arrest disposition	None	Mar. '74[a]	None
Citizen complaints (totals of FI and other by beat and month	Apr. '73-June '73[b] (3 months)	Sept. '73-May '74 (9 months)	None
Observations of, and subject interviews of sample FI contacts	None	Sept. '73-Feb. '74[c]	None
Counts of investigators' requests to examine FI reports (by investigative unit and month)	None	Sept. '73-May '74 (9 months)	None
Survey of investigations on FI usage	None	March '74	None
Community attitude survey	Aug. '73	None	June '74

[a] Arrests made by officers assigned to study areas.
[b] Summary only; not by month.
[c] Sampled over six months.

V. FINDINGS AND CONCLUSIONS

This chapter presents System Development Corporation's (SDC) findings and conclusions as related to each of the questions posed in the San Diego Police Department's Field Interrogation (FI) study proposal. Supporting data and a brief review of the analysis performed accompany each finding.

QUESTION 1: Do Field Interrogations deter crime? Which types of crime, if any, are affected?

FINDINGS

(1.) *The suspension of Field Interrogations in the No-FI Area was associated in time with a significant increase in the monthly frequency of total suppressible crimes. The resumption of Field Interrogations in the No-FI Area was associated in time with a significant decrease in the monthly frequency of total suppressible crimes.*

(2.) *The monthly frequencies of total suppressible crimes did not change significantly in either the Control or the Special FI Area during the time periods studied.*

(3.) *The evaluation was inconclusive in identifying the specific types of suppressible crimes that appeared to be most influenced by the level of FI activity; however, there were indications that crimes committed by juveniles and young adults may be the most influenced.*

(4.) *The small sample of reporting areas and months was not sufficient to construct a conclusive model of the relationship between the frequencies of Field Interrogations and suppressible crimes. However, the preliminary model tends to indicate that suppressible crimes decline as Field Interrogations are increased from zero to some unknown but relatively low level, after which the deterrent value of additional Field Interrogations may decline sharply.*

SUMMARY OF THE ANALYSIS

The analysis consisted of two methods of comparing the changes that occurred in the frequencies of reported crimes in the three study areas during the course of the FI study, and an initial effort to model the relationship between the frequencies of crimes and Field Interrogations.

The eight specific types of crimes analyzed are those defined as suppressible crimes by the San Diego Police Department: robbery, burglary, grand theft, petty theft, auto theft, assault/battery, sex crimes, and malicious mischief/disturbances. With three minor exceptions, these reported crime types are as defined in the FBI's *Uniform Crime Reporting Handbook* (July 1966): (1) *criminal homicides* are excluded from San Diego's suppressible Part I crimes list; (2) San Diego includes *other sex offenses* along with the Part I crime of *forcible rape*, as *sex offenses*; and (3) the Part II crimes of *vandalism* and *disorderly conduct* are grouped into the San Diego reporting category of *malicious mischief/disturbances*. Suppressible Part I crimes, plus *malicious mischief/disturbances*, are referred to in this analysis as total suppressible crimes.

The monthly reports of Field Interrogations, each of the eight specific types of crime, total Part I suppressible crimes, and total suppressible crimes were tabulated for each study area for the Pre-experimental, Experimental, and Post-experimental time periods. These data were then analyzed to identify changes in frequencies of reported Field Interrogations and crimes, and possible relations between the two types of reports.

ANALYSIS DETAILS

(1.) Changes in the monthly mean frequencies of reported crimes and Field Interrogations

The first analysis consisted of comparing the monthly mean numbers of crimes and Field Interrogations reported in each area before, during, and after the active field phase of the FI experiment. Since the raw totals of reports showed a wide month-to-month variation, an analysis approach was chosen to minimize the influence of exceptionally high or low months of reported crimes and Field Interrogations. The technique employed was the standard *t* test of the differences between means. These tests were conducted individually for each of the eight specific types of suppressible crime, for the total of the seven Part I suppressible crimes, and for the total of all suppressible crimes. These tests were also made for reported Field Interrogations, but only for the Experimental and Post-experimental periods, since monthly data were not available for the Pre-experimental period.

Briefly, this analysis produced these findings: first, both total suppressible crimes and Part I suppressible crimes increased significantly in the No-FI Area during the period when Field Interrogations were suspended. When Field Interrogations were resumed there, a significant decrease was observed in both total suppressible crimes and Part I suppressible crimes. These findings support the hypothesis that *some* FI activities—as opposed to *none*—have a deterrent effect on suppressible crimes.

Second, the analysis of specific types of suppressible crimes in the No-FI Area showed that only malicious mischief/disturbances demonstrated a significant increase during the period when Field Interrogations were suspended, and only petty theft showed a statistically significant decrease when Field Interrogations were resumed. However, all specific crime types except assaults increased in the No-FI Area during the period when Field Interrogations were suspended, and all specific crime types except assault and grand theft decreased when Field Interrogations were resumed. The magnitudes and monthly patterns of these changes were most apparent for burglary, petty theft, and malicious mischief/disturbances. Since the test for statistical significance is particularly stringent for small samples, it appears likely that extended study periods would have produced significant results for burglary, petty theft and malicious mischief/disturbances.

Third, there were no significant increases or decreases in individual or combined suppressible crimes in either the Control or Special FI Areas. Although the individual types and aggregates of suppressible crimes showed changes between study periods, neither the magnitude nor patterns of these changes were as consistent as those of the No-FI Area. Field Interrogations increased significantly in the Special FI Area between the Experimental and Post-experimental periods, but were not significantly changed in the Control Area.

Table 5 presents the results of this analysis for the eight individual types of crime. Table 6 presents the results for the two summations of Part I suppressible crimes and for total suppressible crimes, along with the changes that occurred in the frequencies of FI reports. Changes are reported as significant only when *p* = .05 or less (*p* is a measure of the probability that the changes could be due to chance alone). Tables 7, 8, and 9 present the monthly totals of suppressible crimes, Field Interrogations, and arrests by study period for the Control Area, for the Special FI Area, and for the No-FI Area, respectively.

(2.) Relative changes in the frequencies of reported suppressible crimes

The analysis as described above showed that the suspension and later resumption of FI activities in the No-FI Area were associated in time with significant and substantial (20 percent or more) increases and decreases in monthly mean Part I and total suppressible crime reports, while changes in these totals were minor and not significant in the other two areas.

The next analysis task undertaken was to examine the relative changes in crime frequencies that occurred among paired study areas from one time period to the next. For example, the analysis compared the Control and No-FI Areas' individual contributions to their combined total number of burglary reports during the Pre-experimental period with each area's contribution to their combined total of burglary reports during the Experimental period. This analysis approach was included as another method for comparing the effects of alternative FI policies and practices on reported crimes and for attempting to isolate the specific crime types most influenced by FI activities.

Comparisons were made for total suppressible crimes; for all Part I crimes; for the separate components of Part I crimes (robberies, burglaries, grand thefts, petty thefts, auto thefts, assaults, and sex crimes); and for the non-Part I crime malicious mischief/disturbances. For each comparison, the

Table 5

MONTHLY MEAN NUMBERS OF SUPPRESSIBLE CRIMES BY CRIME TYPE, STUDY AREA, AND STUDY PERIOD, PLUS SIGNIFICANCE OF CHANGES BETWEEN STUDY PERIODS

CRIME TYPE	CONTROL AREA					NO-FI					SPECIAL FI AREA				
	MONTHLY MEANS			SIGNIFICANCE OF CHANGE		MONTHLY MEANS			SIGNIFICANCE OF CHANGE		MONTHLY MEANS			SIGNIFICANCE OF CHANGE	
	Pre	Exp	Post	Pre to Exp	Exp to Post	Pre	Exp	Post	Pre to Exp	Exp to Post	Pre	Exp	Post	Pre to Exp	Exp to Post
Robbery	2.0	2.2	1.6	NS	NS	.07	1.2	0.4	NS	NS	1.6	1.6	2.2	NS	NS
Burglary	15.0	12.2	7.8	NS	NS	18.7	27.4	22.4	NS	NS	20.1	19.6	19.8	NS	NS
Grand Theft	2.1	2.8	3.2	NS	NS	1.9	2.8	2.8	NS	NS	1.9	2.9	3.0	NS	NS
Petty Theft	17.9	20.9	20.2	NS	NS	32.7	40.3	27.6	NS	(<.01)	26.3	29.9	26.0	NS	NS
Auto Theft	2.6	2.4	3.0	NS	NS	4.7	6.0	5.2	NS	NS	4.3	3.0	1.4	NS	NS
Assault	0.9	1.9	2.6	NS	NS	3.3	3.2	4.2	NS	NS	2.7	3.1	3.0	NS	NS
Sex Crime	0.4	0.4	0.2	NS	NS	1.1	2.2	0.6	NS	NS	0.9	0.2	1.6	NS	NS
Malicious Mischief/ Disturbances	7.9	9.2	10.0	NS	NS	11.6	20.7	20.0	(<.02)	NS	7.3	9.1	11.8	NS	NS

Pre = Pre-experimental period; Exp = Experimental period; Post = Post-experimental period

NS = Not significant at .05 level of probability.

(<.01) = Less than 1 chance in 100 that change was due to chance alone.

(<.02) = Less than 2 chances in 100 that change was due to chance alone.

NOTE: Significance tests were made using the standard *t* test of the differences between means.

29

Table 6
MONTHLY MEAN NUMBERS OF REPORTING PART I SUPPRESSIBLE CRIMES,
TOTAL SUPPRESSIBLE CRIMES, AND FIs BY STUDY PERIOD AND STUDY AREA

PART I SUPPRESSIBLE CRIMES

Study Areas	Pre-experimental Time Period (7 months)	Experimental Time Period (9 months)	Post-experimental Time Period (5 months)	Differences and Significances[a] Between Periods	
				Pre-experimental to Experimental	Experimental to-Post-experimental
Control	40.9	42.9	38.6	+ 2.0 (NS)	- 4.3 (NS)
Special FI	57.7	60.2	56.6	+ 2.5 (NS)	- 3.6 (NS)
No-FI	63.1	83.2	63.2	+ 20.1 p=.02	- 20.0 p=.05

TOTAL SUPPRESSIBLE CRIMES[b]

Study Areas	Pre-experimental	Experimental	Post-experimental	Pre to Experimental	Experimental to Post
Control	48.7	52.1	48.6	+ 3.4 (NS)	- 3.5 (NS)
Special FI	65.0	69.3	68.4	+ 4.3 (NS)	- 0.9 (NS)
No-FI	74.7	103.9	81.2	+ 29.2 p=.01	- 22.7 p=.05

FIELD INTERROGATIONS[c]

Study Areas	Pre-experimental	Experimental	Post-experimental	Pre to Experimental	Experimental to Post
Control	17.0	22.7	14.0	+ 5.7 (NA)	- 8.7 (NS)
Special FI	15.0	48.3	88.0	+ 33.3 (NA)	+39.7 p=.05
No-FI	24.0	0.0	49.2	- 24.0 (NA/D)	+ 49.2 (NA/D)

(NS) = Not significant.
(NA) = Not applicable due to lack of data for Pre-experimental period.
(NA/D) = Not applicable. Significance forced by experimental design.
[a] Tests of statistical significance of the differences between monthly means were made using the standard t test.
[b] Comprises Part I plus malicious mischief/disturbances.
[c] One-month sample only.

data were arranged in a two-by-two contingency table designed to compare relative differences between time periods and between areas. For example,

AREA	TOTAL REPORTED SUPPRESSIBLE CRIMES	
	Pre-experimental Period	Experimental Period
Control	341	469
Special FI	455	624

Notice that this form of analysis, unlike the t test of monthly means, does not consider month-to-month variation in the frequencies of reported crimes, but deals only with the totals for each study period.

Sixty separate tables were created to compare the areas and time periods for all crime types. The Yates chi square test was used to analyze the contingency tables when the number of observations was over 50; Fisher's test was used for smaller samples.

The following discussion of findings resulting from the analysis performed is divided into three parts: (1) findings with regard to changes occurring between the Pre-experimental and Experimental periods; (2) findings resulting from changes between the Experimental and Post-experimental periods; and (3) conclusions based on the combined findings.

30

Table 7

NUMBERS OF REPORTED SUPPRESSIBLE CRIMES, FIELD INTERROGATIONS, AND ARRESTS FOR THE CONTROL AREA

Project Periods By Month	Robbery	Burglary	Grand Theft	Petty Theft	Auto Theft	Assault	Sex Crimes	Total Part I	Malicious Mischief/ Disturbance	Total Crimes	Total FIs	Total Arrests[a]
Pre-experimental Period												
Feb. '73	2	3	3	17	1	0	0	26	7	33	—	—
Mar.	6	14	5	12	6	1	2	46	0	46	—	—
Apr.	2	17	2	16	1	0	1	39	6	45	—	—
May	0	16	1	15	2	2	0	36	10	46	17[b]	14
June	2	16	3	24	2	1	0	48	12	60	—	37
July	0	29	1	22	6	0	0	58	9	67	—	35
Aug.	2	10	0	19	0	2	0	33	11	44	—	39
Total	14	105	15	125	18	6	3	286	55	341	17[b]	125
Monthly Mean	2.0	15.0	2.1	17.9	2.6	0.9	0.4	40.9	7.9	48.7	17[b]	31.2
Experimental Period												
Sept.	2	8	1	15	3	2	1	32	4	36	20	23
Oct.	1	21	4	21	2	4	0	53	6	59	16	30
Nov.	3	16	2	19	1	4	0	45	11	56	17	19
Dec.	3	11	3	28	4	2	1	52	9	61	17	29
Jan. '74	1	13	3	14	4	0	0	35	13	48	36	31
Feb.	1	10	3	26	1	0	1	42	12	54	18	16
Mar.	4	12	3	27	2	2	1	51	10	61	33	29
Apr.	4	9	2	21	2	0	0	38	11	49	20	32
May	1	10	4	17	3	3	0	38	7	45	27	18
Total	20	110	25	188	22	17	4	386	83	469	204	227
Monthly Mean	2.2	12.2	2.8	20.9	2.4	1.9	0.4	42.9	9.2	52.1	22.7	25.2
Post-experimental Period												
June	0	8	5	18	10	1	0	42	11	53	31	31
July	2	6	3	16	0	4	0	31	13	44	16	15
Aug.	2	5	1	28	0	1	1	38	8	46	1	26
Sept.	4	8	6	21	2	7	0	48	11	59	11	29
Oct.	0	12	1	18	3	0	0	34	7	41	11	15
Total	8	39	16	101	15	13	1	193	50	243	70	116
Monthly Mean	1.6	7.8	3.2	20.2	3.0	2.6	0.2	38.6	10.0	48.6	14.0	23.2

[a] Prior to May 1973, the San Diego Police Department did not include juvenile arrests in its manually compiled tabulation of total arrests by beat, nor were separate tabulations available.

[b] FI totals for the Pre-experimental period are estimated based on a one-month sample. Totals are actual for the other periods.

31

Table 8
NUMBERS OF REPORTED SUPPRESSIBLE CRIMES, FIELD INTERROGATIONS, AND ARRESTS FOR THE SPECIAL FI AREA

Project Periods By Month	Robbery	Burglary	Grand Theft	Petty Theft	Auto Theft	Assault	Sex Crimes	Total Part I	Malicious Mischief/ Disturbance	Total Crimes	Total FIs	Total[a] Arrests
Pre-experimental Period												
Feb. '73	1	17	1	21	0	2	0	42	6	48	—	—
Mar.	4	23	2	25	4	1	0	59	9	68	—	—
Apr.	0	16	0	30	4	2	0	52	6	58	—	—
May.	2	19	3	18	7	4	4	57	10	67	15[b]	25
June	1	18	3	29	4	2	0	57	12	69	—	47
July	1	28	3	27	6	4	0	69	4	73	—	34
Aug.	2	20	1	34	5	4	2	68	4	72	—	23
Total	11	141	13	184	30	19	6	404	51	455	15[b]	129
Monthly Mean	1.6	20.1	1.9	26.3	4.3	2.7	1.0	57.7	7.3	65.0	15[b]	32.2
Experimental Period												
Sept.	1	13	6	13	2	2	0	37	11	48	26	29
Oct.	1	18	1	27	4	6	0	57	4	61	55	78
Nov.	1	20	8	24	4	1	0	58	8	66	29	63
Dec.	1	19	2	19	1	2	0	44	10	54	27	66
Jan. '74	1	9	2	24	5	3	0	44	6	50	34	51
Feb.	2	16	2	33	4	1	0	58	10	68	48	48
Mar.	4	22	2	51	5	0	0	84	10	94	92	70
Apr.	2	23	0	34	2	4	0	65	12	77	72	70
May	1	36	3	44	0	9	2	95	11	106	52	65
Total	14	176	26	269	27	28	2	542	82	624	435	540
Monthly Mean	1.6	19.6	2.9	29.9	3.0	3.1	0.2	60.2	9.1	69.3	48.3	60.0
Post-experimental Period												
June	2	20	4	27	1	7	0	60	17	77	59	77
July	3	20	1	37	3	2	4	69	12	81	70	73
Aug.	1	17	5	28	1	1	0	53	10	63	40	75
Sept.	3	25	3	17	1	3	0	52	9	61	132	60
Oct.	2	17	2	21	1	2	4	49	11	60	139	76
Total	11	99	15	130	7	15	8	283	59	342	440	361
Monthly Mean	2.2	19.8	3.0	26.0	1.4	3.0	1.6	56.6	11.8	68.4	88.0	72.2

[a] Prior to May 1973, the San Diego Police Department did not include juvenile arrests in its manually compiled tabulation of total arrests by beat, nor were separate tabulations available.

[b] FI totals for the Pre-experimental period are estimated based on a one-month sample. Totals are actual for the other periods.

Table 9

NUMBERS OF REPORTED SUPPRESSIBLE CRIMES, FIELD INTERROGATIONS, AND ARRESTS FOR THE NO-FI AREA

Project Periods By Month	Robbery	Burglary	Grand Theft	Petty Theft	Auto Theft	Assault	Sex Crimes	Total Part I	Malicious Mischief/ Disturbance	Total Crimes	Total FIs	Total[a] Arrests
Pre-experimental Period												
Feb. '73	0	17	2	40	4	4	0	67	16	83	—	—
Mar.	0	25	4	47	3	4	1	84	7	91	—	—
Apr.	2	14	1	38	5	0	2	62	9	71	—	—
May	0	17	0	31	1	4	2	55	11	66	24[b]	44
June	3	24	1	28	4	7	1	68	15	83	—	39
July	0	12	2	34	7	1	1	57	13	70	—	41
Aug.	0	22	3	11	9	3	1	49	10	59	—	29
Total	5	131	13	229	33	23	8	442	81	523	24[b]	129
Monthly Mean	0.7	18.7	1.9	32.7	4.7	3.3	1.1	63.1	11.6	74.7	24[b]	32.2
Experimental Period												
Sept.	1	11	1	33	3	2	4	55	16	71	0	29
Oct.	1	30	1	31	13	3	2	81	11	92	0	59
Nov.	1	18	2	41	0	2	4	68	24	92	0	40
Dec.	1	46	0	43	14	1	0	105	39	144	0	36
Jan. '74	2	28	9	54	5	4	1	103	26	129	0	48
Feb.	2	37	1	40	0	4	1	85	21	106	0	38
Mar.	0	32	6	38	4	4	6	90	15	105	0	46
Apr.	0	20	2	42	2	6	1	73	15	88	0	38
May	3	25	3	41	13	3	1	89	19	108	0	32
Total	11	247	25	363	54	29	20	749	186	935	0	366
Monthly Mean	1.2	27.4	2.8	40.3	6.0	3.2	2.2	83.2	20.7	103.9	0	40.7
Post-experimental Period												
June	1	25	5	31	2	5	0	69	22	91	62	45
July	0	23	5	28	8	6	2	72	18	90	56	46
Aug.	1	19	0	24	9	4	0	57	23	80	22	30
Sept.	0	23	3	36	2	1	0	65	23	78	56	24
Oct.	0	22	1	19	5	5	1	53	14	67	50	34
Total	2	112	14	138	26	21	3	316	100	406	246	169
Monthly Mean	0.4	22.4	2.8	27.6	5.2	4.2	0.6	63.2	20.0	81.2	49.2	33.8

[a] Prior to May 1973, the San Diego Police Department did not include juvenile arrests in its manually compiled tabulation of total arrests by beat, nor were separate tabulations available.

[b] FI totals for the Pre-experimental period are estimated based on a one-month sample. Totals are actual for the other periods.

33

- Pre-experimental to Experimental period findings
  (a) Three comparisons between the Control Area and the No-FI Area yielded significant results. The No-FI Area experienced a significantly larger share of total crimes, total Part I crimes, and burglaries during the Experimental period than it had during the Pre-experimental period. The differences between the Control and No-FI Areas in total crimes were significant at the .01 level of significance in total Part I crimes, at the .025 level; and in burglaries, at the .002 level. Differences for the other components of Part I crimes were not significant at the .05 level. Excluding burglaries, results for Part I crimes were not significant at the .05 level; however, results remained significant for total crimes.

  Results for burglaries were investigated further to determine if extraneous factors may have influenced the statistical comparison. This investigation, conducted by the department's project coordinator, revealed that an apparently well-organized group of juveniles, indigenous to the No-FI Area, was released from juvenile hall in mid-December but were re-incarcerated in January as a result of their involvement in multiple burglaries during the month of December.

  On the basis that the December burglaries in the No-FI Area were exceptional for reasons not associated with the experiment, the December data were excluded from the Experimental period for both areas and the chi-square test used to compare burglaries in the No-FI and Control Areas was repeated. The increase in burglaries in the No-FI Area, as compared with the Control Area, was found to still be significant at the .01 level.
  (b) Four comparisons between the No-FI and Special FI Areas yielded significant results. The No-FI Area received a significantly larger share of total suppressible crimes (.002); of suppressible Part I crimes (.01); burglaries (.025); and sex crimes (.05).
  (c) There were no significant results in the comparisons of the Control and Special FI Areas. This was true for aggregate crimes and for each component crime listed above.

- Experimental period to Post-experimental period findings
  (a) Comparisons between the Control and No-FI Areas failed to reveal any statistically significant differences at the .05 level, although total suppressible crimes approached being significantly lower in the former No-FI Area. (The chi-square value was 3.12 as compared with the 3.84 required at the .05 level of probability.)
  (b) Comparisons between the No-FI and Special FI Areas, however, showed significant differences with regard to total crimes, total Part I crimes, and sex crimes. In each of these cases, the No-FI Area showed reduced frequencies of these reported crimes.
  (c) Comparison between the Control and Special FI Areas showed a single significant difference: the relative frequencies of sex crimes had decreased in the Control Area while increasing in the Special FI Area.

- Conclusions based on the chi-square frequency analysis

  In general, the results of this analysis tend to confirm the results of the prior tests made of monthly mean crimes, which showed that the suspension of Field Interrogations in the No-FI Area was associated with significant increases in the aggregates of suppressible crimes (Part I crimes and total suppressible crimes).

  The frequency analysis also supported (but less strongly) the earlier indications that total suppressible crimes decreased significantly in the No-FI Area when Field Interrogations were resumed.

  Both forms of analysis tended to indicate that the special FI training given to officers working the Special FI Area and their increased use of Field Interrogation failed to influence reported crime rates in that area.

  The two forms of analysis were individually and jointly inconclusive in identifying the specific types of suppressible crimes that were most influenced by FI activities. In the No-FI Area, monthly reports of malicious mischief/disturbances increased significantly when Field Interrogations were suspended, but failed to decrease significantly when they were resumed. Monthly reports of petty thefts decreased significantly when Field Interrogations were resumed but had not increased significantly when Field Interrogations had been suspended. The relative frequency of burglary reports in the No-FI Area increased significantly when Field

Table 10

RELATIVE FREQUENCIES OF REPORTED CRIMES DURING PRE-EXPERIMENTAL AND EXPERIMENTAL PERIODS BY AREA

Comparison 1: Control vs. Spec. FI

CRIME TYPE	AREA	Pre-experim.	Experim.	Total	Significance
Total Crimes	Control	341	469	810	
	Spec. FI	455	624	1079	
	Total	796	1093	1889	Not significant at .05
Total Part I Crimes	Control	286	386	672	
	Spec. FI	404	542	946	
	Total	690	928	1618	Not significant at .05
Robberies	Control	14	20	34	
	Spec. FI	11	14	25	
	Total	25	34	59	Not significant at .05
Burglaries	Control	105	110	215	
	Spec. FI	141	176	317	
	Total	246	286	532	Not significant at .05
Grand Thefts	Control	15	25	40	
	Spec. FI	13	26	39	
	Total	28	51	79	Not significant at .05

Comparison 2: Control vs. No-FI

CRIME TYPE	AREA	Pre-experim.	Experim.	Total	Significance
Total Crimes	Control	341	469	810	
	No-FI	523	935	1458	
	Total	864	1404	2268	Significant at .01 (chi square = 8.29)
Total Part I Crimes	Control	286	386	672	
	No-FI	442	749	1191	
	Total	728	1135	1863	Significant at .025 (chi square = 5.13)
Robberies	Control	14	20	34	
	No-FI	5	11	16	
	Total	19	31	50	Not significant at .05
Burglaries	Control	105	110	215	
	No-FI	131	247	378	
	Total	236	357	593	Significant at .002 (chi square = 11.0)
Grand Thefts	Control	15	25	40	
	No-FI	13	25	38	
	Total	28	50	78	Not significant at .05

Comparison 3: No-FI vs. Spec. FI

CRIME TYPE	AREA	Pre-experim.	Experim.	Total	Significance
Total Crimes	No-FI	523	935	1458	
	Spec. FI	455	624	1079	
	Total	978	1559	2537	Significant at .002 (chi square = 10.1)
Total Part I Crimes	No-FI	442	749	1191	
	Spec. FI	404	542	946	
	Total	846	1291	2137	Significant at .01 (chi square = 6.67)
Robberies	No-FI	5	11	16	
	Spec. FI	11	14	25	
	Total	16	25	41	Not significant at .05
Burglaries	No-FI	131	247	378	
	Spec. FI	141	176	317	
	Total	272	423	695	Significant at .025 (chi square = 6.58)
Grand Thefts	No-FI	13	25	38	
	Spec. FI	13	26	39	
	Total	26	51	77	Not significant at .05

Table 10 (continued)

RELATIVE FREQUENCIES OF REPORTED CRIMES DURING PRE-EXPERIMENTAL AND EXPERIMENTAL PERIODS BY AREA

CRIME TYPE	AREA	PERIOD			AREA	PERIOD			AREA	PERIOD		
		Pre-experim.	Experim.	Total		Pre-experim.	Experim.	Total		Pre-experim.	Experim.	Total
Petty Thefts	Control	125	188	313	Control	125	188	313	No-FI	229	363	592
	Spec. FI	184	269	453	No-FI	229	363	592	Spec. FI	184	269	453
	Total	309	457	766	Total	354	551	905	Total	413	632	1045
	Not significant at .05				Not significant at .05				Not significant at .05			
Auto Thefts	Control	18	22	40	Control	18	22	40	No-FI	33	54	87
	Spec. FI	30	27	57	No-FI	33	54	87	Spec. FI	30	27	57
	Total	48	49	97	Total	51	76	127	Total	63	81	144
	Not significant at .05				Not significant at .05				Not significant at .05			
Assaults	Control	6	17	23	Control	6	17	23	No-FI	23	29	52
	Spec. FI	19	28	47	No-FI	23	29	52	Spec. FI	19	28	47
	Total	25	45	70	Total	29	46	75	Total	42	57	99
	Not significant at .05				Not significant at .05				Not significant at .05			
Sex Crimes	Control	3	4	7	Control	3	4	7	No-FI	8	20	28
	Spec. FI	6	2	8	No-FI	8	20	28	Spec. FI	6	2	8
	Total	9	6	15	Total	11	24	35	Total	14	22	36
	Not significant at .05				Not significant at .05				Not significant at .05			
Malicious Mischief/ Disturbances	Control	55	83	138	Control	55	83	138	No-FI	81	186	267
	Spec. FI	51	82	133	No-FI	81	186	267	Spec. FI	51	82	133
	Total	106	165	271	Total	136	269	405	Total	132	268	400
	Not significant at .05				Not significant at .05				Not significant at .05			

NOTE: The significance test used for all contingency tables with more than 50 observations was Yates chi square test; for 50 or less observations, Fisher's exact test was used.

36

Table 11

RELATIVE FREQUENCIES OF REPORTED CRIMES DURING EXPERIMENTAL AND POST-EXPERIMENTAL PERIODS BY AREA

Total Crimes

AREA	Experim.	Post	Total	AREA	Experim.	Post	Total	AREA	Experim.	Post	Total
Control	469	243	712	Control	469	243	712	No-FI	935	406	1341
Spec. FI	624	342	966	No-FI	935	406	1341	Spec. FI	624	342	966
Total	1093	585	1678	Total	1404	649	2053	Total	1559	748	2307
Not significant at .05				Not significant at .05				Significant at $<.01$ (chi square= 6.7)			

Total Part I Crimes

AREA	Experim.	Post	Total	AREA	Experim.	Post	Total	AREA	Experim.	Post	Total
Control	386	193	579	Control	386	193	579	No-FI	749	316	1065
Spec. FI	542	283	825	No-FI	749	316	1065	Spec. FI	542	283	825
Total	928	476	1404	Total	1135	509	1644	Total	1291	594	1890
Not significant at .05				Not significant at .05				Significant at .05 (chi square - 4.6)			

Robberies

AREA	Experim.	Post	Total	AREA	Experim.	Post	Total	AREA	Experim.	Post	Total
Control	20	8	28	Control	20	8	28	No-FI	11	2	13
Spec. FI	14	11	25	No-FI	11	2	13	Spec. FI	14	11	25
Total	34	19	53	Total	31	10	41	Total	25	13	38
Not significant at .05				Not significant at .05				Not significant at .05			

Burglaries

AREA	Experim.	Post	Total	AREA	Experim.	Post	Total	AREA	Experim.	Post	Total
Control	110	39	149	Control	110	39	149	No-FI	247	112	359
Spec. FI	176	99	275	No-FI	247	112	359	Spec. FI	176	99	275
Total	286	138	424	Total	357	151	508	Total	423	211	634
Not significant at .05				Not significant at .05				Not significant at .05			

Grand Thefts

AREA	Experim.	Post	Total	AREA	Experim.	Post	Total	AREA	Experim.	Post	Total
Control	25	16	41	Control	25	16	41	No-FI	25	14	39
Spec. FI	26	15	41	No-FI	25	14	39	Spec. FI	26	15	41
Total	51	31	82	Total	50	30	80	Total	51	29	80
Not significant at .05				Not significant at .05				Not significant at .05			

37

Table 11 (continued)

RELATIVE FREQUENCIES OF REPORTED CRIMES DURING EXPERIMENTAL AND POST-EXPERIMENTAL PERIODS BY AREA

CRIME TYPE	AREA	PERIOD			AREA	PERIOD			AREA	PERIOD		
		Experim.	Post	Total		Experim.	Post	Total		Experim.	Post	Total
Petty Thefts	Control	188	101	289	Control	188	101	289	No-FI	363	138	501
	Spec. FI	269	130	399	No-FI	363	138	501	Spec. FI	269	130	399
	Total	457	231	658	Total	551	239	790	Total	632	268	900
		Not significant at .05				Not significant at .05				Not significant at .05		
Auto Thefts	Control	22	15	37	Control	22	15	37	No-FI	54	26	80
	Spec. FI	27	7	34	No-FI	54	26	80	Spec. FI	27	7	34
	Total	49	22	71	Total	76	41	117	Total	81	33	114
		Not significant at .05				Not significant at .05				Not significant at .05		
Assaults	Control	17	13	30	Control	17	13	30	No-FI	29	21	50
	Spec. FI	28	15	43	No-FI	29	21	50	Spec. FI	28	15	43
	Total	45	28	73	Total	46	34	80	Total	57	36	93
		Not significant at .05				Not significant at .05				Not significant at .05		
Sex Crimes	Control	4	1	5	Control	3	1	5	No-FI	20	3	23
	Spec. FI	2	8	10	No-FI	20	3	23	Spec. FI	2	8	10
	Total	6	9	15	Total	24	4	28	Total	22	11	33
		Significant at P=.05				Not significant at .05				Significant at P=.05		
Malicious Mischief/ Disturbances	Control	83	50	133	Control	83	50	133	No-FI	186	90	276
	Spec. FI	82	59	141	No-FI	186	90	276	Spec. FI	82	59	141
	Total	165	109	274	Total	269	140	409	Total	268	140	417
		Not significant at .05				Not significant at .05				Not significant at .05		

NOTE: The significance test used for all contingency tables with more than 50 observations was Yates chi square test; for 50 or less observations, Fisher's exact test was used.

Interrogations were suspended, but failed to decrease significantly when Field Interrogations were resumed.

However, the crimes of malicious mischief/disturbances, petty theft, and burglary share some common attributes that may help to identify the probable influence that FI activities may have on the frequencies of suppressible crime: (1) these crimes are committed more frequently by juveniles and young adults than by offenders in other age groups; (2) these crimes are most often committed by small groups of offenders rather than by individuals; and (3) these offenses occur most frequently during the daytime and in residential areas. These same attributes coincide with the conditions and circumstances that surrounded the majority of the 639 Field Interrogations conducted in the study area during the nine-month Experimental period. Thus,

(a) Almost half (48.4 percent) of FI subjects were juveniles (data were not kept for young adults).

(b) The majority (56.5 percent) of FI encounters were of two or more individuals.

(c) The majority (56.2) of Field Interrogations were conducted during daylight hours, and all three study areas consisted primarily of residential developments.

Table 10 presents the actual chi-square contingency tables used for the evaluation of changes in the relative frequencies of reported crimes by study area, comparing Pre-experimental and Experimental periods. Table 11 reports the chi-square tables for crime types, by study area, and compares Experimental and Post-experimental periods.

(3.) Modeling the statistical relationship between Field Interrogations and crimes

A standardized correlation/regression analysis of the three study beats used in the analysis was

Table 12
RELATIVE MEASUREMENT OF FIELD INTERROGATIONS AND TOTAL CRIMES
BY MONTH AND AREA

DATE	NO-FI AREA		CONTROL AREA		SPECIAL FI AREA	
	Total FIs (Z_1 score)	Total Crimes (Z_2 score)	Total FIs (Z_1 score)	Total Crimes (Z_2 score)	Total FIs (Z_1 score)	Total Crimes (Z_2 score)
Sept. '73	- .70	1.21	.05	- 1.95	- 1.04	- 1.32
Oct.	- .70	- .18	- .39	1.07	- .21	- .50
Nov.	- .70	- .18	- .28	.68	- .96	- .19
Dec.	- .70	- 2.35	- .28	1.33	- 1.02	- .94
Jan. '74	- .70	1.62	1.80	- .38	- .82	- 1.19
Feb.	- .70	.50	- .17	.41	- .41	- .06
Mar.	- .70	.45	1.47	1.33	.84	1.57
Apr.	- .70	- .38	.50	- .24	.27	.50
May	- .70	.59	.81	- .77	- .30	2.32
June	1.78	- .23	1.25	.28	- .10	.50
July	1.53	- .28	- .39	- .90	.21	.75
Aug.	.18	- .77	- 2.03	- .64	- .64	- .38
Sep.	1.53	- .87	- .94	1.07	1.99	- .50
Oct.	1.30	- 1.40	- .94	- 1.30	2.19	- .57
Relative Mean	0.00	0.00	0.00	0.00	0.00	0.00
Relative Standard Deviation	1.00	1.00	1.00	1.00	1.00	1.00
Original Mean	17.57	95.79	19.57	50.86	62.50	69.00
Original Standard Deviation	25.04	20.55	9.14	7.61	34.97	15.92
$rz_1 z_2$ (With one month lag)	-.550		-.188		.155	
$rz_1 z_2$ (No lag)	-.473		.122		.177	

39

performed in order to initiate the study of a model depicting the relationship between Field Interrogations and crimes.

The monthly figures for total Field Interrogations and total crimes were transformed into standardized Z scores, based on the monthly means and standard deviations of each beat during the entire time period between September and October 1974 (see Table 12). This approach was designed to permit comparison of data from separate areas by adjusting for individual area differences.

The Z score transformations were studied for time-lag effects, as well as for study area relationships. The time-lag investigation showed a tendency for the one-month lagged relationship in each study area to be more negative than the unlagged relationship. (A negative relationship is one in which crimes decrease as Field Interrogations increase.)

The correlation relationships which express the changes in the frequencies of crimes which were associated with changes in the frequencies of Field Interrogations were as follows:

AREA	NO LAG	1-MONTH LAG
N (No-FI)	-.47	-.55
C (Control)	+.12	-.55
S (Special FI)	+.18	+.15

These figures express the change that occurred, as measured in standard deviations of the monthly crime rates, when monthly Field Interrogations were increased by one standard deviation. For example, using the data shown in Table 12 we see that an FI increase of one standard deviation in the No-FI Area would be 25.04 Field Interrogations. One month after such an increase, crimes changed by -.55 standard deviations in crimes (or -.55 x 20.55). Thus an increase of approximately 25 Field Interrogations per month resulted in a decrease of approximately 12 crimes the following month.

The lagged relationships for individual areas ranged from a high correlation of -.55 in the No-FI Area to +.15 in the Special FI Area.

To achieve more statistical stability in the model, the paired Z scores for the three areas were combined into one analysis, as shown in Figure 2. The simple linear model for this analysis can be described by the equation $Z_{TC} = -.18Z_{FI}$, which indicates that there is a tendency for total crimes (TC) to decrease .18 of a standard deviation below their norm, one month after total Field Interrogations are increased by one standard deviation above their area norm.

The relationship discussed here is not sufficiently conclusive to establish a general model describing the impact of Field Interrogations on crimes, but it does tend to support the hypothesis that Field Interrogations provide a deterrent to suppressible crimes, and suggests that additional modeling investigations in representative areas be performed. If this is attempted, the data design should allow for a sufficient number of paired observation points from a larger representative sample of beats. In addition, the impact of other potential variables, such as types of FI subjects and situations, should be simultaneously explored. It would seem likely that the deterrent effects of Field Interrogations may decrease as the appropriateness of increased FI contacts decrease. If this proves to be true, it would support the position of those FI advocates who maintain that FI quotas should not be established.

QUESTION 2: Do Field Interrogations either directly or indirectly lead to arrests?

FINDINGS

(1.) *The monthly frequencies of total arrests in the study areas did not appear to have been significantly changed by the FI experiment.*

(2.) *Departmentwide patrol officers attribute 17 percent of their total arrests to contacts that began as Field Interrogations.*

(3.) *Taking into account that most (83 percent) of the arrests in the department arise from other than FI activities (such as radio calls), and that more than 98 percent of Field Interrogations reported do not result in arrests, it is clear that whatever effects Field Interrogations have in suppressing crime stem mainly from the Field Interrogation process itself.*

(4.) *The quality of arrests resulting from FI contacts is slightly lower than for arrests in other circumstances. Thirty percent of the subjects arrested as a result of a Field Interrogation are held-to-answer as compared with 38 percent for arrests in all other circumstances.*

(5.) *While the majority (62 percent) of the subjects of Field Interrogations were not residents of the area where they were stopped, the majority (57 percent) of arrest subjects were local residents.*

(6.) *There were no significant differences with regard to race/ethnicity, age, or sex between the subjects of Field Interrogations and subjects of arrests made by the Special FI group. However, the Control group arrested significantly more Blacks, and significantly fewer Mexican-Americans and males, than they Field Interrogated. There were no indications of race discrimination, through unjustified arrests, by either group.*

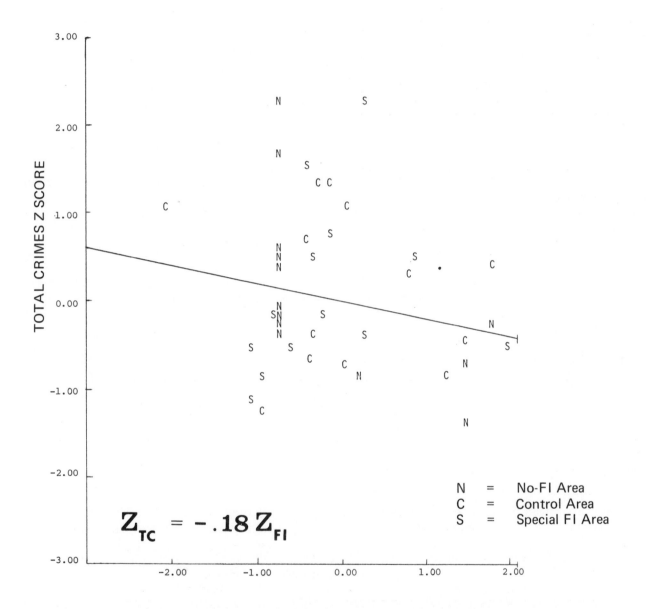

Figure 2
COMBINED RELATIONSHIP OF FIELD INTERROGATIONS
AND TOTAL CRIMES

(7.) *The majority (69 percent) of investigators reported that FI reports were useful in case investigations, and 37 percent reported one or more case clearances in the prior six months through the use of Field Interrogation information.*

(8.) *Because of the manual filing system used for FI reports, only 15.5 percent of the written reports were examined by investigators.*

SUMMARY OF THE ANALYSIS

This analysis reported earlier that monthly mean totals of suppressible crimes had increased significantly in the No-FI Area when Field Interrogations were suspended and had decreased significantly when they were resumed. Suppressible crimes had also increased then decreased in the other two study areas during the same time periods, but the changes were minor and not significant. Here, the basic analysis is directed, first, at measuring the changes that occurred in the frequencies of total arrests made in the study areas. Second, the analysis uses a small sample of arrests to perform a number of comparisons of arrest details.

ANALYSIS DETAILS

(1.) Changes in the monthly mean totals of arrests

Using the monthly numbers of total arrests made in each study area (as previously shown in Tables 7, 8, and 9) standard *t* tests for the differences in means were used to determine whether or not any of the areas exhibited statistically significant changes in monthly total arrests. The results of this analysis are shown in Table 13.

Table 13
MONTHLY MEAN TOTAL ARRESTS MADE IN STUDY AREAS BY PERIOD,
INCLUDING DIFFERENCE IN MEANS AND SIGNIFICANCE OF DIFFERENCES BY PERIOD

STUDY AREA	PERIOD			DIFFERENCES AND SIGNIFICANCE[a]			
	Pre-exper.	Exper.	Post-exper.	Per-exper. to Exper.		Exper. to Post-exper.	
				Diff.	Signif.	Diff.	Signif.
Control	17.6	25.2	23.2	+ 6.0	NS[b]	− 2.0	NS
Special FI	32.2	60.0	72.2	+ 27.8	.01	+ 12.2	NS
No-FI	32.2	40.7	33.8	+ 8.5	NS	− 6.9	NS

[a] Significance as measured by the standard *t* test of means.
[b] NS = Not significant.

Monthly mean total arrests increased in all areas (including the No-FI Area) between the Pre-experimental and Experimental time periods, but the only significant increase was in the Special FI Area.

Between Experimental and Post-experimental periods, there were no significant changes in monthly mean arrests in any study area. Arrests continued to increase in the Special FI Area but declined in the other two areas.

The suspension and then resumption of Field Interrogations in the No-FI Area were not associated with significant changes in the monthly mean number of total arrests in the area, although, as previously shown, they were associated with significant changes in suppressible crime rates.

The question of whether or not the additional FI training given to patrol officers in the Special FI Area or the officers' increased use of Field Interrogations are associated with the significant increase in total arrests in that area during the Experimental period, is examined next.

(2.) Total arrests and arrests made by assigned officers

The analysis described above dealt with changes in total arrests made in each study area. The next question addressed was the extent to which the patrol officers assigned to the study areas were responsible for the arrests made there. Table 14 presents the results of a one-month sample (March 1974) of total arrests by area.

Table 14
ONE-MONTH SAMPLE OF TOTAL ARRESTS BY AREA,
AND ARRESTS MADE BY ASSIGNED PATROL OFFICERS

STUDY AREA	TOTAL ARRESTS MADE IN AREA	ARRESTS MADE BY ASSIGNED PATROL OFFICERS	
		(N)	(%)
Control	29	5	17.2
Special FI	70	16	22.9
No-FI	46	12	26.1
Total	145	33	22.8

It appears doubtful that the experimental conditions had much influence on the total arrests made in the study areas, since only 22.8 percent of the total arrests made in the areas were made by the patrol officers assigned there. Chi-square tests of the data were performed to determine if there were any significant differences among study areas in ratios of arrests made by assigned officers, to total arrests made in the area. The results, shown in Table 15, reveal that there were no significant differences.

Thus the experimental conditions were not associated with statistically significant differences among areas in this regard.

A related question was posed: *Since the officers assigned to the study areas were making only about one-fourth or less of the total arrests made in their assigned patrol areas, how many more arrests were they making elsewhere?* Again, the same one-month sample (March 1974) of arrest details was examined. Table 16 shows that each group of officers was making far more arrests off its assigned beat than on it.

Results of chi-square tests to determine any significant differences among the officer groups (see Table 17) showed that the officers assigned to the Control Area made significantly fewer of their own total arrests in their assigned area than did the other two groups of officers. This finding suggests that the Control officers may have been more mobile than the other two officer groups.

In order to help understand the arrest findings, it is important to remember, first, that San Diego patrol officers are normally not restricted to their assigned beats; second, that calls for service on a beat are frequently answered by officers not assigned there; and third, that there were no experimental controls placed on the mobility of officers assigned to the study areas. Experimental controls were related only to the conduct of Field Interrogations, and restricted the officers not assigned to the study areas from conducting Field Interrogations in these areas. Additionally, all patrol officers were restricted from conducting Field Interrogations in the No-FI Area during the Experimental period.

The preceding analysis of arrest data has shown that the only significant change in total arrests made in each area was the increase that occurred in the Special FI Area. Officers assigned to that area, however, accounted for only 22.9 percent of the total arrests made there, and actually made the majority (78.1) of their own total arrests in other areas.

Based on these findings, it appears that neither of the experimental variables (the suspension of Field Interrogations, and the use of specially trained officers to conduct Field Interrogations) had a significant influence on the total number of arrests made in the study areas.

The remainder of the analysis of arrests focuses on differences in arrest circumstances, dispositions, and characteristics of arrest subjects.

(3.) Circumstances leading to arrests

A planned Field Interrogation can become an arrest if the contact results in the patrol officer identifying a wanted person or in finding other grounds (reasonable cause) for making an arrest. In these cases only the arrest, and not the Field Interrogation, is reported. In order to determine how frequently planned Field Interrogations result in arrests, and to measure the influence of other types of police activity that lead to arrests, the following analysis was undertaken.

The data for this analysis came from the six-month period (December 1973 through May 1974)

43

Table 15
DIFFERENCES AMONG STUDY AREAS IN ARRESTS MADE BY
ASSIGNED OFFICERS AND IN TOTAL ARRESTS MADE IN STUDY AREAS

AREA	BY ASSIGNED OFFICER	BY OTHER OFFICERS	ARREST TOTALS
Control	5	24	29
No-FI	12	34	46
Total	17	58	75
		$x^2 = .80(NS)$	

AREA	BY ASSIGNED OFFICER	BY OTHER OFFICERS	ARREST TOTALS
Control	5	24	29
Special FI	16	54	70
Total	21	78	99
		$x^2 = 0.38(NS)$	

AREA	BY ASSIGNED OFFICER	BY OTHER OFFICERS	ARREST TOTALS
Special FI	16	54	70
No-FI	12	34	46
Total	28	88	116
		$x^2 = 0.15(NS)$	

NS = Not significant
NOTE: Chi-square test of arrest data for March 1974.

44

Table 16
ONE-MONTH SAMPLE OF TOTAL ARRESTS BY BEAT PATROL
OFFICERS AND THOSE ARRESTS MADE ON THEIR ASSIGNED BEATS

OFFICERS' ASSIGNED AREA	TOTAL ARRESTS BY OFFICER GROUP	ARRESTS ON ASSIGNED BEAT	
		(N)	(%)
Control	98	5	5.1
Special FI	76	16	21.1
No-FI	82	12	14.6
Total	256	33	12.9

when the San Diego Police Department utilized a special printed version of its standard arrest report. Each arresting officer was asked to checkmark a box to indicate the police event that immediately preceded each arrest. The possible choices were Field Interrogation, radio call, traffic, warrant, and other. Other includes arrests resulting from on-view crimes, stakeouts, bar checks, persons under the influence of alcohol or drugs, search warrants, prostitution, bookmaking, *hot sheet* pickups, juvenile pickups (including curfew violations), and so on.

As Table 18 shows, the FI process contributed 17 percent of all arrests, departmentwide. Table 19 presents a comparable analysis of arrests made by officers assigned to the FI study areas. The major difference between the two tables appears to be that the suspension of Field Interrogations in the No-FI Area caused proportional increases in two arrest categories—radio call, and other arrests.

During the six-month period covered by Table 18 there were 20,787 Field Interrogations recorded departmentwide. During the same period, 392 arrests (17.1 percent of 2,294) were made that began as Field Interrogations. Accordingly, of the total of 21,179 Field Interrogations conducted, less than two percent resulted in arrests. When it is additionally considered that 83 percent of arrests during the period arise from other than FI activities, it seems clear that whatever effects Field Interrogations have in suppressing crime stem mainly from the FI process itself.

The data in Tables 18 and 19 also help to partially explain the high mobility of patrol officers, as reflected in the previous analysis of arrests described earlier. Radio calls, which frequently take patrol officers away from their assigned beats, account for a large percentage of the arrests. Unfortunately, data were not available to examine the possibility that control officers responded to fewer of the calls on their assignment beat than did the other two groups—a finding that might account for the differences shown earlier in Table 16.

Since patrol officers attribute a sizable percentage (17 percent departmentwide) of their arrests to contacts that began as Field Interrogations, the next question explored in the analysis was the relationship between the crime suspicions that led officers to conduct and report Field Interrogations, and the actual crime charges entered on arrest reports.

The FI report form used in San Diego provides a box for the patrol officer to record suspicions concerning each FI subject's potential criminal activity. Entries are written in, usually in the form of the applicable criminal code. For example, 459 would indicate a potential burglary suspect. The same codes are used to designate arrest charges on arrest reports.

An analysis of the crime potential entries made in FI reports during the nine months of the active phase of the FI study showed no major differences between regularly trained (Control) officers and officers who received special supplemental FI training (Special FI) with regard to these entries (see Table 20).

Also, all arrest reports completed by officers assigned to the three study areas during a one-month sample period were reviewed for the arrest charge recorded by the arresting officer. Table 21 shows the percentages of arrested subjects by arrest charge.

When comparing the officers' judgment as to the potential criminal activity of FI subjects with the officer's recorded arrest charges of arrest subjects, the major difference is that officers frequently record the subject's potential criminal activity as that of a burglary suspect (more than 40 percent), whereas actual arrests on burglary charges are recorded considerably less frequently (10-15 percent).

During March 1974, the officers assigned to the Control Area reported that 15 of their 98 total arrests resulted from planned Field Interrogations, and the officers assigned to the Special FI Area

Table 17
DIFFERENCES AMONG STUDY AREAS IN TOTAL ARRESTS BY OFFICER GROUP AND IN ARRESTS MADE ON ASSIGNED BEATS

GROUP	ARRESTS OFF BEAT	ARRESTS ON BEAT	TOTAL ARRESTS
Control	93	5	98
No-FI	70	12	82
Total	163	17	180

$x^2 = 4.74$ (sig. $<.05$)

GROUP	ARRESTS OFF BEAT	ARRESTS ON BEAT	TOTAL ARRESTS
Control	93	5	98
Special FI	60	16	76
Total	153	21	174

$x^2 = 10.26$ (sig. $<.01$)

GROUP	ARRESTS OFF BEAT	ARRESTS ON BEAT	TOTAL ARRESTS
Special FI	60	16	76
No-FI	70	12	82
Total	130	28	158

$x^2 = 1.74$(NS)[a]

[a] NS = Not significant.
NOTE: Chi-square test of arrest data for March 1974.

Table 18
DEPARTMENTWIDE ARRESTS BY
IMMEDIATELY PRECEDING POLICE EVENT

OFFICER GROUP	TOTAL NUMBER OF ARRESTS	PRECEDING POLICE EVENT (%)				
		FI	Radio Call	Traffic	Warrant	Other
Total city	2294	17.1	32.0	20.7	3.7	26.5

NOTE: Arrest data for period December 1973 through May 1974.

Table 19
ARRESTS MADE BY OFFICERS ASSIGNED TO THE STUDY AREAS,
BY IMMEDIATELY PRECEDING POLICE EVENT

OFFICERS' AREA ASSIGNMENT	TOTAL ARRESTS	PRECEDING POLICE EVENT (%)				
		FI	Radio Call	Traffic	Warrant	Other
Control	98	15.3	39.2	17.7	6.3	21.14
Special FI	76	14.5	33.3	19.0	3.2	30.0
No-FI	82	0.0	42.9	12.2	0.0	44.9
Total	256	10.2	38.5	16.3	3.2	31.9

NOTE: Arrest data for March 1974.

reported that 11 of their 76 total arrests resulted from planned Field Interrogations. Details of these FI arrests were analyzed to identify the specific arrest charges. These data are presented in Table 22.

Only one of the 26 FI arrests was charged for a crime type (robbery) listed as a suppressible crime. On the basis of this admittedly small sample, it appears that any deterrent value that FI arrests may have in reducing suppressible crimes is not closely related to the specific charges of these arrests.

(4.) Quality of Field Interrogations and other arrests

One measure of the quality of arrests made by patrol officers is the percentage of arrest subjects that are held-to-answer, that is, their cases are accepted for prosecution or other forms of adjudication. Table 23 compares a one-month sample of arrests made by officers assigned to the three study areas, in terms of this measure of the quality of arrests. The table also compares the quality of arrests that resulted from planned Field Interrogations with those that resulted from all other police activities, including answering calls for service, serving warrants, traffic enforcement, and so on.

On the basis of this limited sample, it appears that officers given the special FI training had the highest quality of both FI-related and other arrests. As might be expected, the general quality of FI arrests is less than that for other arrests. The latter includes those resulting directly from complainants' calls for service, from warrants, and from criminal activity observed directly by the patrol officers (traffic, under-the-influence, and on-view arrests). Also notice that the quality of other arrests made by No-FI officers is not much lower than that of Control officers. This would suggest that arrests were not used as substitutes for Field Interrogations.

(5.) Characteristics of arrest and FI subjects compared
  • Mobility of arrest and FI subjects
    A one-month sample of arrest reports and FI reports made by officers assigned to study areas were compared to determine the percentages of each type of report that pertained to individuals who lived in the same area where the arrest or Field Interrogation occurred. The sample included only the Control and Special FI Areas, since no field Interrogations were being conducted in the No-FI Area. Moreover, the sample was limited to a single month because of the clerical complexity of performing the necessary matching of addresses with study areas, for both the location of the stop and the residential address of the arrest subjects.

47

Table 20

STUDY AREA FIELD INTERROGATION SUBJECTS BY SUSPECTED CRIME CATEGORIES

STUDY AREA	CRIME CATEGORY (%)							
	Burglary	Robbery	Grand Theft	Petty Theft	Auto Theft	Assault Battery	Narcotics	Other or Blank
Control (N=204)	42.9	13.4	3.2	6.9	2.0	2.4	19.8	9.3
Special FI (N=435)	44.5	17.9	2.3	5.2	2.9	2.3	14.5	10.4
No-FI[a] (N=0)	—	—	—	—	—	—	—	—

N = Total number of FIs reported in study areas.

[a] No Field Interrogations were conducted in the No=FI Area.

NOTE: Data are for the period September 1973 through May 1974.

Table 21

ARRESTS BY ARREST CHARGE

STUDY AREA	CRIME CATEGORY (%)							
	Burglary	Robbery	Grand Theft	Petty Theft	Auto Theft	Assault Battery	Narcotics	All Other Charges
Control (N=98)	10.4	7.3	0.0	10.4	1.0	4.2	18.8	50.0
Special FI (N=76)	13.2	6.6	0.0	11.8	5.3	7.9	27.6	27.6
No-FI (N=82)	15.9	11.0	0.0	8.5	2.4	13.4	13.4	35.4

N = Total arrests made by officers assigned to study areas.

NOTE: Data are for March 1974 sample of all arrests made by officers assigned to study areas.

Table 22
SPECIFIC CHARGES OF ARRESTS RESULTING FROM PLANNED
FIELD INTERROGATIONS

SPECIFIC ARREST CHARGE	ARRESTS BY CONTROL OFFICERS		ARRESTS BY SPECIAL FI OFFICERS		COMBINED ARRESTS BY BOTH GROUPS	
	(N)	(%)	(N)	(%)	(N)	(%)
Narcotics	3	20.0	6	54.5	9	34.6
Curfew	5	33.3	1	9.1	6	23.1
Drunk	2	13.3	1	9.1	3	11.5
Robbery	1	6.7	0	0	1	3.8
Loaded Gun	1	6.7	0	0	1	3.8
Miscellaneous[a]	3	20.0	3	27.3	6	23.1
Total FI Arrests	15	100%	11	100%	26	100%

[a] Miscellaneous charges included 2 mandatory traffic arrests, 1 traffic warrant, 1 failure-to-support warrant, 1 contempt warrant and 1 illegal driver's license.

NOTE: Data are from March 1974 sample of arrests made by officers assigned to the control and Special FI Areas.

Table 23
INITIAL ARREST DISPOSITIONS FOR FIELD INTERROGATION ARRESTS
AND OTHER ARRESTS MADE BY OFFICERS ASSIGNED TO STUDY AREAS

AREA	TOTAL NUMBER	HELD-TO-ANSWER[a] (N)	HELD-TO-ANSWER (%)
Control			
FI arrests	15	4	26.7
Other arrests	83	31	37.3
Special FI			
FI arrests	11	4	36.4
Other arrests	65	28	43.1
No-FI			
FI arrests	0	0	0
Other arrests	82	30	36.6
All areas			
Total FI arrest	26	8	30.8
Total other arrests	230	89	38.7
Total arrests	256	97	37.9

[a] Held-to-answer are adult cases accepted by the district attorney or city attorney plus juvenile cases accepted by the probation department and/or juvenile hall.

NOTES: FI arrests are those arrests reported as resulting from a planned Field Interrogation.

Data are from March 1974.

As Table 24 shows, the majority of the subjects of Field Interrogations were not local residents; however, a slight majority of the persons arrested in the study area were local residents. The selection of FI subjects who are not local residents is consistent with the theoretical tendency for Field Interrogations to be applied to persons whose presence might create suspicion.

Table 24
MOBILITY OF ARREST AND FIELD INTERROGATION SUBJECTS

OFFICERS' ASSIGNMENT AREA	ARREST SUBJECTS[a]			FI SUBJECTS[b]		
	Total	Local Residents	%	Total	Local Residents	%
Control	5	0	0.0	33	11	33.3
Special FI	16	12	75.0	92	36	39.1
Total	21	12	57.1	125	47	37.6

[a] Includes only subjects arrested in the study areas by officers assigned there.
[b] All subjects of FI reports made in the study areas; that is, all FI reports were made by the officers assigned to the areas.
NOTE: Data are from March 1974 sample of arrests and Field Interrogations made in study areas by assigned officers.

Table 25
COMPARISON OF SELECTED SUBJECT CHARACTERISTICS FROM SEPARATE DATA SOURCES
FOR THE CONTROL AND EXPERIMENTAL AREAS

DATA SOURCE	JUVENILE		MALE		BLACK		MEXICAN-AMERICAN	
	Control (%)	Special FI (%)	Control (%)	Special FI (%)	Control (%)	Special FI (%)	Control (%)	Special FI (%)
1970 Census Control (N=8,725) Exper. (N=7,412)	37.9	49.6 (<.01)	48.4	48.9	17.5	4.5 (<.01)	12.2	22.1 (<.01)
			[<.01]—	[<.01]—	[<.01]—	[<.01]—		
FI Reports[a] Control (N=204) Exper. (N-435)	32.4	55.9 (<.01)	99.0	97.5	34.3	54.7 (<.01)	21.6	15.6
			[<.01]—		[<.01]—		[<.01]—	
Arrest Reports[b] Control (N=98) Exper. (N=76)	42.5	47.2	74.4	92.1 (<.01)	62.8	44.7	6.4	11.8

( ) = Statistically significant differences between areas.
[ ] = Statistically significant differences between data sources.
[a] Nine-month sample of all FI reports written in the study areas.
[b] One-month sample of arrests made by officers assigned to the study areas.

- Personal characteristics of arrest and FI subjects

  In advance of the San Diego FI study, there was concern among those involved in the study planning that patrol officers might be misusing the FI contact as a means of hassling certain minority segments of the population. As a result of these concerns, data were gathered to permit a series of comparisons of the characteristics of FI subjects with those of arrested persons and of the general population.

  As Table 25 shows, percentages of male and Black FI subjects are markedly higher than those of the general population; however, the characteristics of FI subjects more closely resemble those of arrest subjects. These data are derived from various sources but, in each case, compare the Special FI Area with the Control Area.

50

Statistical analysis of the data showed that the Special FI Area had significantly (<.01) more juveniles and Blacks, and fewer Mexican-Americans, than did the Control Area, according to the 1970 census. However, data from the community survey samples (see Appendix B, Tables B-1 and B-3) indicate that the percentage of Blacks in the Control Area had probably increased to 13-18 percent by 1974. The percentage of Mexican-Americans (as measured by the community survey samples) showed an increase in the Special FI Area, to be 14-16 percent. On this basis, the two areas appeared to be very comparable in terms of the numbers of these two minorities.

With regard to FI subjects, the Special FI officers field interrogated significantly (<.01) more juveniles and Blacks than did the Control officers.

The only significant differences between the two groups of officers (in terms of the characteristics of the persons they arrested) was that the Control group arrested a smaller percentage of males than did the Special FI group.

When comparing the characteristics of FI subjects with those of arrested persons, the significant differences were that the Control officers arrested significantly *more* Blacks than they had field interrogated, and arrested significantly *fewer* males and Mexican-Americans than they had field interrogated.

On the basis of these findings, it appears that Special FI officers tended to select FI subjects whose age and ethnic characteristics were essentially the same as those of the persons arrested. The Control group (which did not receive the Special FI training) tended to field interrogate males and Mexican-Americans more frequently than they arrested them, and Blacks less frequently than they arrested them.

The above analysis led to a second question: Were unjustified arrests used to hassle minorities? The same one-month sample of arrests made by officers assigned to the two study areas was used to compare the quality of arrests by race/ethnicity groups. Table 26 presents the findings, and shows that arrested Whites and Blacks were essentially equally likely to be held-to-answer. By the same measure, arrested Mexican-Americans were the least likely group to have been hassled by unjustified arrests, since more than 60 percent were held-to-answer by authorities other than the police.

(6.) Use of Field Interrogation reports by investigators
During the nine months of the Experimental period, the total San Diego Police Department generated slightly more than 29,000 FI reports. A daily summary of new FI reports were generated by keypunching and listing a brief subset of the reported data items. These daily summary listings were provided to investigators and patrol supervisors. For investigators or others to have access to the complete FI reports, an FI document request form had to be completed for each report requested. A total of 4,495 document request forms were received, including 743 from external agencies. The total document-request-to-file size ratio was thus about 15.5 percent. Assuming there were no duplicate requests, this means that one FI report in seven was examined by investigators. Table 27 shows the requests to examine FI reports made by each of the investigating units, by month.

- Investigator questionnaire
  In March 1974, a questionnaire was distributed to 147 officers working in various investigative units. Ninety-three questionnaires were returned, for a response rate of 63.2 percent. The results of this questionnaire are presented in Table 28. Of 93 respondents to the first item, 59 percent indicated that they regularly attempt to use FI data to assist them in investigation, while an additional 34 percent use FI information but do so infrequently.
  FI information was considered helpful by 69 percent of the respondents. This response is relatively consistent with the fact that 59 percent of the investigators regularly use FI data.
  Somewhat inconsistent with the foregoing responses was the finding that only 37 percent of the investigators could attribute any specific case clearances during the preceding six months directly to FI information.
  It was the opinion of 72 percent of the respondents that information captured on the department's new FI form was of greater assistance to investigators than that previously collected.

51

Table 26

QUALITY OF ARREST BY RACE/ETHNICITY OF ARREST SUBJECTS

RACE/ETHNICITY OF ARREST SUBJECTS

OFFICERS ASSIGNMENT AREA	Whites			Blacks			Mexican-Americans			Other		
	Arrested (N)	Held-to-Answer (N)	(%)	Arrested (N)	Held-to-Answer (N)	(%)	Arrested (N)	Held-to-Answer (N)	(%)	Arrested (N)	Held-to-Answer (N)	(%)
Control	27	11	40.7	59	21	35.6	7	2	28.6	5	1	20.0
Special FI	32	10	31.3	34	13	38.2	9	8	88.9	1	1	100.0
Both Officer Groups	59	21	37.1	83	34	36.5	16	10	62.5	6	2	33.3

NOTE: Data are from March 1974 sample of all arrests made by officers assigned to study areas.

Table 27

REQUESTS TO EXAMINE FIELD INTERROGATION SOURCE DOCUMENTS

NUMBER OF REQUESTS BY MONTH

INVESTIGATING UNIT	Sept. '73	Oct. '73	Nov. '73	Dec. '73	Jan. '74	Feb. '74	Mar. '74	Apr. '74	May '74	Total	%
Auto Theft	11	19	17	18	19	16	25	22	13	160	3.6
Burglary	113	104	80	82	140	116	111	83	141	970	21.6
Community Relations	1	2	–	–	–	–	–	–	–	3	0.0
Forgery	11	45	57	60	32	31	70	48	59	413	9.2
Fraud	8	2	9	8	5	4	–	–	4	40	0.1
Homicide and Sex Crimes	45	32	26	47	35	25	30	37	48	325	7.2
Intelligence (ISU)[a]	12	25	67	54	38	21	25	29	21	292	6.5
Juvenile	13	3	12	5	2	–	2	4	6	48	1.1
Narcotics	17	4	5	2	20	2	3	1	4	58	1.3
Patrol	84	68	55	154	110	83	104	95	89	842	18.7
Robbery	12	5	8	71	68	16	66	77	75	398	8.9
Traffic	3	14	5	3	5	3	–	7	6	46	1.0
Vice (PIU)[b]	16	12	22	13	13	24	29	7	21	157	3.5
Other[c]	58	43	66	69	72	108	134	109	84	743	16.5
Total	404	378	430	586	559	449	599	519	571	4495	100
Mean Daily Requests	13.5	12.2	14.3	18.9	18.0	16.0	19.3	16.7	18.4	16.4	–

[a] ISU = Internal support unit
[b] PIU = Public inspection unit
[c] Other includes other police or regulatory agencies such as Department of Defense, Internal Revenue Service, FBI, district attorney, etc.
NOTE: Data are from September 1973 through May 1974.

Finally, with regard to investigator use of the daily summary tabulation that was provided to investigators during the Experimental period, 44 percent *occasionally* found the printout useful while only 14 percent *often* found it useful. Subsequent discussions with some of the respondents revealed that the primary criticism of the tabulation was that the printout was difficult to read and that the FI slips themselves were not readily available. Fifty-one percent of the investigators viewed the summary tabulation of FI information, coupled with the new filing system employed by the records section, as an improvement in the availability and accessibility of the data.

Coded printouts, such as the one provided for the summary tabulation, were considered too complicated to read, and it was even more time consuming to locate and extract data from source documents. All investigators indicated that on-line computer access to FI data, and the capability to search the file for individuals or vehicles matching specified time, place, and other characteristics, would greatly increase their use of FI data.

Burglary investigators reported using FI information more frequently, and clearing more cases using this information, than did any other investigative unit.

TABLE 28
USE OF FIELD INTERROGATIONS BY INVESTIGATORS AS
REPORTED ON MARCH 1974 QUESTIONNAIRE

RESPONDENTS' INVESTIGATION UNIT / RESPONSES	Burglary	Homicide/ Sex Crime	Auto Theft	Forgery	Juvenile	Robbery Task Force	ISU[a]	PIU[b]	Total	% of Response[c]	Responses To Item
Use FIs?											
Yes, regularly	14	7	3	6	6	5	2	12	55	59	93
No	2	–	–	1	1	1	–	1	6	7	
Infrequently	8	10	2	4	3	–	–	5	32	34	
FI Helpful?											
Yes	18	10	3	6	5	5	2	15	64	69	93
No	6	7	2	5	5	1	–	3	29	31	
Case Clearance?											
0	14	11	2	8	4	2	2	12	55	63	87
1–2	4	4		2	5	1			16	18	
3–4	4	1						1	6	7–	
5–6	2	1			1			2	6	7–	
7–8						1			1	1+	
9 or more			3						3	3+	
New Form?											
More useful	13	7	4	9	7	6	2	17	65	72	90
No difference	6	2	1	2	–	–	–	1	12	13+	
Less useful	3	8	–	–	2	–	–	–	13	14+	
Printout Useful?											
Never	8	7	5	8	2	1	–	7	38	42	90
Occasionally	15	8	–	3		3	2	9	40	44	
Often	–	1	–	–	8	2	–	1	12	14	
Improved Availability?											
Yes	10	6	4	6	5	5	1	10	47	51	93
No	4	7	1	2	2	1	–	2	19	20	
Don't know	10	4	–	3	3	–	1	6	27	29	

[a] ISU = Internal support unit.
[b] PIU = Public inspection unit.
[c] Percentages rounded to nearest integer.

- Requests to conduct Field Interrogations

  The investigative supplement form is used by investigators to request that patrol officers conduct special Field Interrogations in connection with a specific investigation. Fifty-nine supplement forms, issued March 1-May 30, 1974, were reviewed to determine how extensively the form was used by investigators (see Table 29). According to the findings: (a) five of the nine investigative units used this vehicle as a possible source of additional information; (b) 36 individual officers made requests (This figure may be misleading because at least four of the requesting officers were sergeants who may have requested information for investigators working in their units, and because many investigators work in teams, so that one could request information for use by the team.); and (c) more than 50 percent of the requests were initiated by the burglary investigation unit.

  Investigators who requested patrol officers to conduct special Field Interrogations were interviewed by the project evaluator and by the department monitor to determine the success rate of acquiring meaningful, useful data via the investigative supplemental form. Specific successes were difficult to identify. At best, three case solutions and arrests were directly attributable to FI data so obtained. However, several investigators stated that FI data had contributed, to a small degree, to the clearing of some cases.

- Summary of investigators' use of FI reports

  Briefly, a majority (69 percent) of the investigators expressed the opinion that FI reports were of assistance to them in the conduct of case investigations, and 37 percent could directly attribute one or more case clearances in the prior six months to FI information. All the investigators who were surveyed indicated a need for a computer-based FI-file-search capability.

Table 29

REQUESTS FOR FIELD INTERROGATIONS FROM INVESTIGATIVE SUPPLEMENTS

| REQUESTING UNIT | INFORMATION PROVIDED IN REQUESTS FOR FIs[a] | | TOTALS | | NUMBER OF OFFICERS REQUESTING |
	Person Description	Persons and/or Vehicle Descriptions	(N)	(%)	
Burglary	19	25	44	53.7	18
Robbery	5	4	9	11.0	6
Homicide & Sex Crimes	9	6	15	18.3	4
Forgery	–	3	3	3.6	2
Juvenile	4	7	11	13.4	6
Total	37	45	82	100	36
Percent	45.1	54.9	100		

[a] There were no requests based on descriptions of situations or areas.
NOTE: Data are for March 1, 1974 through May 30, 1974.

QUESTION 3: Is there a direct relationship between Field Interrogations and negative police-community relationships?

FINDINGS

(1.) *FI activities do not have a major effect on police-community relations in San Diego.*
(2.) *The majority of citizens in all three study areas accept Field Interrogations as a legitimate and properly conducted police activity, and feel that an appropriate amount of police time is devoted to the practice.*

(3.) *The majority of all citizens who were the subjects of FI contacts felt that the contact was justified and properly conducted. No citizen complaints resulted from FI contacts made in either the Control or Special FI Areas.*

(4.) *The actual increase in crime in the No-FI Area during the suspension of Field Interrogations there is reflected in an increase in citizen fear of crime, in increased citizen experience with crime, and in opinions that the crime rate was increasing.*

(5.) *The special FI training program officers patrolling the Special FI Area and the officers' increased use of Field Interrogations had no significant effect on public attitudes regarding the performance of patrol officers there, other than an increase in the minority of survey respondents who felt that police were spending too much time in questioning and searching suspicious persons.*

(6.) *The significant changes in public attitudes in the Control Area were an increase in the percentage of citizens who thought crime in the area was decreasing, even though the percentage with personal experience with crime, as victims or witnesses, increased.*

(7.) *Observation of FI encounters by SDC observers failed to identify any major differences in the Field Interrogations conducted by Control and Special FI officers. However, FI subjects reacted more favorably to interrogations conducted by Special FI officers than by Control officers.*

SUMMARY OF THE ANALYSIS

Several data sources were analyzed to determine the effect of alternative FI practices on police-community relations. Changes in public attitudes were assessed through community surveys. Citizen complaints were analyzed for their relationship to FI practices. FI contacts were observed in the field by trained observers, and the subjects of FI contacts were interviewed for their reactions.

ANALYSIS DETAILS

(1.) Analysis of the community surveys

Impacts of the experimental factors on community attitudes toward criminal activities, and on relations with police, were measured by analysis of the results of the two community attitude surveys.

Table 30
COMPOSITE VARIABLES USED IN ANALYSIS OF COMMUNITY SURVEYS

VARIABLES	COMPONENT QUESTIONS	ATTITUDE MEASURED
Fear of Crime	5-8	Assessment of risk of crime (against person or property, day or night) in the neighborhood.
Opinions on Crime Trends	13, 14	View of crime rate (against person or property) in past year compared with previous years.
Security Efforts	15, 16	Public efforts to protect home or person during the past year.
Personal Acquaintance with Police	26-28	Personal acquaintance with police by name, or as a friend or relative.
Police Use of Time	29-37	Citizen satisfaction with the amount of time that police spend on various patrol functions.
Police Rights	41-44	Assessment of the right of police to stop and search citizens under various circumstances.
Experience with Crime	50-53	Citizen's reported experience with crime during the past year (either direct or as onlooker, crime against persons or property).
Satisfaction with Police Responses to Calls for Service	58, 59	Satisfaction with length of time it took police to arrive, and with performance of police after arrival.
Police-initiated Contacts	60, 63, 66	Citizen's experience with traffic tickets, stops or searches for other possible violations, or witnessing of stops or searches.

The first of these was conducted in 1973 before the experiment commenced, and the second was conducted one year later, at the close of the experiment. The number of completed interviews per area averaged 180 in the 1973 survey and 202 in the 1974 survey. This number was relatively small for purposes of detecting and comparing changes between areas.

Because of this, an attempt was made to increase the sensitivity of the analysis by combining questions according to subject matter. Nine new variables were created (see Table 30), each of which was the sum of responses to component questions that measured attitudes.

Clearly, each composite variable had a broader range of possible values than any of its components; these numerical values are measures of intensity of attitude when each component question is given equal weight. The composite variable was not created for an individual who did not respond or whose response to a component question was "don't know."

For each of these composite variables, two-way analysis of variance statistical techniques (ANOVA)[8] were employed to assess differences in responses between surveys and between areas. Comparisons were made between responses of the two surveys within each area, and also between areas for each survey. In addition, for each of the three ethnic and the four age subgroups, changes between surveys within each area were analyzed by means of this statistical technique. A summary of some of the findings follows.

- Fear of crime
  Between the two surveys, fear of crime did not change significantly in the Control Area. In the other areas, however, changes were significant but in opposite directions: Fear of crime declined in the Special FI Area, but increased in the No-FI Area. Initially, there were no significant differences among the areas with regard to this variable, but differences were significant (at the .03 level) in the second survey, as indicated by analysis of variance tests.

- Opinions on crime trends
  In all three areas, opinions about neighborhood crime trends during the past year compared with previous years, changed significantly. In the No-FI Area, there was an increase in the proportion that believed either violent or property crimes had become worse. In contrast, opinion changes in the other two areas moved in the reverse direction: a larger proportion reported no crime or less crime. In the No-FI Area, citizen opinion reflected the statistically significant increases in burglaries and in malicious mischief/disturbances in the No-FI Area, relative to the Control Area.
  Areas differed significantly (<.01 level) on this variable, in both the first and second surveys. During both surveys, respondents in the Control Area were the most pessimistic about crime trends.

- Security efforts
  Between the two surveys in the No-FI and Control Areas, there were no significant changes in the proportion of residents who increased their personal or home security. In the Special FI Area, on the other hand, this proportion decreased significantly. The latter finding is consistent with the community's decreased fear of crime, noted earlier.
  Initially there was no significant difference among the areas; however, in the second survey differences were significant (<.01 level). In the second survey, significantly fewer respondents in the Special FI Area reported actions to improve their security.

- Personal acquaintance with police
  Between surveys, there were no significant changes in acquaintance with police in either the Control or the No-FI Area. However, in the Special FI Area acquaintance with police declined significantly. This was due primarily to a decline in the proportion that had good friends or relatives on the police force.
  Tests showed no significant difference among areas for the first survey, but significant (.03 level) differences for the second. The difference in the second survey is accounted for

---

[8] ANOVA is the name of a series of computer programs.

by a decline in the number of respondents in the Special FI Area who had friends or relatives on the police force.

- Police use of time
  In none of the three areas was there any significant change between surveys in residents' attitudes toward police use of time as measured by this combined variable. However, it is of interest to note that in the case of one component of this variable—time spent on questioning and searching suspicious persons—a significantly (.01 level) larger minority in the Special FI Area reported too much time being spent in the second survey, than did in the first (44 percent as against 23 percent). This is consistent with the finding that the number of Field Interrogations performed in the Special FI Area was considerably greater than in the Control Area. Differences were not significant for the other two areas.
  Differences among the areas were not significant for either the first or the second survey.

- Rights of police
  There were no significant changes between surveys in attitudes toward the rights of police to stop and search citizens in any of the areas. With the exception of the 20-34 age group in the Control Area, the attitude of no age group in any of the three areas changed significantly. The 20-30 age group showed a shift toward more agreement with the rights of police. There were no significant changes for any of the three ethnic groups residing within the areas.
  At the time of the first survey, there were significant (.03 level) differences among the areas in attitudes toward rights of police. These were also present in the second survey (.03 level). Since the differences remained constant, however, they do not appear to be related to the FI experiment. In both surveys, the respondents from the Special FI Area indicated less agreement with the rights of police than did respondents from the other areas.

- Experience with crime
  Between surveys, reported experience with crime (as victims or observers) increased significantly both in the Control (.03 level) and No-FI (<.01 level) Areas. There was a decrease in the Special FI Area, but it was not significant.
  Analysis of the component questions of this composite variable showed that these changes were due primarily to changes in experience with property crimes. The Control and No-FI Areas had significant increases in the proportions that witnessed property damage to others in the neighborhood; and on the other hand, residents of the Special FI Area reported a significant decrease in property damage to their own households. No other component questions showed significant changes in any of the areas.
  Differences among the areas were significant (<.01 level) in both surveys. In the first survey, the Control Area had the most experience with crime while the Special FI Area had the least experience. In the second survey, the No-FI Area had the most experience, and the other two areas had equivalent experience.

- Satisfaction with police response to calls for service
  Between surveys in the Control and No-FI Areas, dissatisfaction with police response to calls for service increased significantly (<.01 level); but there was no significant change in the Special FI Area. Subgroups for which this change was significant were Whites and the over-50 age category. Although the response differences proved to be significant, the evaluators felt that apparent differences were not related to FI activities. Previous studies in San Diego have shown that a substantial majority of calls for service in any given beat are answered by patrol units assigned to other beats; thus the public reaction to the services provided in the area cannot be linked directly to the performance of officers assigned to patrol a given area.
  In the first survey, differences among areas were not significant; differences were significant (.04 level) in the second survey, however, when respondents from the Special FI Area showed a higher level of satisfaction with police services.

- Contacts initiated by police

  Between surveys, citizens believed that contacts initiated by police decreased significantly in the No-FI Area (.01 level), due primarily to a decrease in traffic citations. In the Control Area, contacts were believed to have decreased but not significantly; however, no change in this composite variable was reported for the Special FI Area. Shifts in response to the component question about being stopped and questioned for non-traffic reasons differed among the areas, though none was significant. In the Control and No-FI Areas, the proportion stopped or who witnessed stops for non-traffic reasons decreased, whereas in the Special FI Area there was a slight increase. This finding is consistent with the distribution of Field Interrogations among the three areas during the course of the experiment.

  Differences among the areas were not significant in either the surveys. Thus, citizens in the study areas showed little awareness of the levels of FI activities in their areas.

Analysis Summary. Table 31 presents a summary of the results of the two-way analysis of variance for each of the nine composite community attitude variables. Table 32 presents a summary of the results of the analysis with regard to age and ethnic groups.

In addition to the analysis of variance statistical tests reported here, multiple regression techniques were also employed. For each of the nine composite attitude variables defined above, a multiple regression equation, using as independent variables, demographic characteristics, time, and area, was calculated. The objective was to determine to what extent variations in the composite attitude variables could be explained by means of variations in the following variables: age, sex, race/ethnicity, survey area (Special FI, No-FI, or Control), and time (first or second year). The square of the multiple correlation coefficient (R^2), which is a measure of the proportion of the variation in the dependent variable that is explained by or may be attributed to variations in the independent variables of the equation, ranged from .01 in the case of security efforts, to .13 for rights of police. Each of the nine regression equations was significant at the .001 level. However, with R^2 values as low as the ones observed (see Table 33), it is clear that these models are not adequate representations of the factors that account for variation in the attitude composite variables. Consequently this analysis was not pursued beyond identifying those independent variables that were most closely correlated to the attitude measures.

(2.) Citizen complaints

No citizen complaints originated in any of the study areas during either the baseline period or the experiment. Table 34 presents the history of citizen complaints against the San Diego Police Department during the Experimental period of the FI study. Summarized, these data illustrate that 65 3.7 percent) of the 1,745 complaints received by the department resulted from FI encounters. Looking at these data from another perspective, only .22 percent of the 29,082 Field Interrogations that were conducted resulted in complaints against the department. None of the 65 FI-associated complaints were against the specially trained officers or the officers working in the Control Area.

Compared with the three-month baseline period, the monthly rate of complaints remained constant (approximately 193 per month), whereas the percentage attributed to Field Interrogations declined from 9 percent to 3.7 percent. Inadequacies of baseline data prohibited investigation of the causes for this decline.

(3.) Observation conclusions

During the course of the 625 hours of observation distributed over 96 shifts, only 79 actual FI encounters were observed. Of these, 37 were performed by Control officers and 42 by Special FI-trained officers. While *observed* encounters averaged .75 per Control shift and .88 per Special FI shift, the average number of encounters per shift (both observed and unobserved) was much less: .21 per Special FI shift and .15 per Control shift. Since observed FI rates were higher than the mean rates for the entire period, it suggests that both groups may have increased either FI activity or reporting when accompanied by observers.

Conferences among the four observers and review of the records of the observations found observers to be in agreement on three conclusions: (1) no discernible group differences were noticed between the approach, techniques, or procedures employed by the Control officers and Special

Table 31
COMMUNITY ATTITUDES BY AREA AND SURVEY, AND SIGNIFICANCE TESTS OF DIFFERENCES

COMPOSITE COMPONENT VARIABLE QUESTIONS	CONTROL AREA		NO FI AREA		SPECIAL FI AREA		ANOVA TEST OF SIGNIFICANCE AMONG AREAS	
	Survey 1	Survey 2	Survey 1	Survey 2	Survey 1	Survey 2	Survey 1	Survey 2
Fear of Crime (5,6,7,8)							NS	.03
Mean	10.1	9.9	9.9	9.1	9.3	10.1		
Standard deviation	3.2	3.5	3.1	3.6	3.3	3.8		
ANOVA (between surveys)	NS[a]		.03		.05			
direction	no change		fear increased		fear decreased			
Opinions of Crime Trend (13,14)							<.01	<.01
Mean	5.6	4.7	4.5	5.8	4.9	4.2		
Standard deviation	1.8	1.8	1.8	1.8	1.9	1.7		
ANOVA (between surveys)	<.01		<.01		<.01			
direction	crime decreasing		crime increasing		crime decreasing			
Security Efforts (15,16)							NS	<.01
Mean	3.3	3.4	3.2	3.2	3.2	3.5		
Standard deviation	.7	.7	.7	.7	.8	.7		
ANOVA (between surveys)	NS		NS		<.01			
direction	no change		no change		decreased effort			
Personal Acquaintance with Police (26,27,28)							NS	.03
Mean	4.8	4.9	5.0	4.9	4.8	5.1		
Standard deviation	.9	.9	.8	.9	.9	.8		
ANOVA (between surveys)	NS		NS		<.01			
direction	no change		no change		acquaint. declined			
Police Use Of Time (29-37)							NS	NS
Mean	19.8	20.2	20.1	20.9	20.5	19.3		
Standard deviation	2.0	2.0	2.4	2.5	2.9	1.8		
ANOVA (between surveys)	NS		NS		NS			
direction	no change		no change		no change			
Rights of Police (41,42,43,44)							.03	.03
Mean	8.6	7.9	8.0	8.4	8.9	8.8		
Standard deviation	3.2	3.2	3.0	3.2	3.2	3.6		
ANOVA (between surveys)	NS		NS		NS			
direction	no change		no change		no change			
Experience With Crime (50,51,52,53)							<.01	<.01
Mean	7.6	7.4	7.4	7.1	7.3	7.4		
Standard deviation	.7	.8	.9	.9	.8	.8		
ANOVA (between surveys)	.03		<.01		NS			
direction	experience increased		experience increased		no change			
Satisfaction with Calls for Service (58,59)							NS	.04
Mean	3.8	5.3	4.4	5.5	4.8	4.5		
Standard deviation	2.2	2.6	2.3	2.5	2.5	2.4		
ANOVA (between surveys)	<.01		<.01		NS			
direction	satisfaction declined		satisfaction declined		no change			
Police Initiated Contacts (60,63,66)							NS	NS
Mean	5.3	5.4	5.3	5.5	5.3	5.3		
Standard deviation	.8	.7	.7	.7	.7	.8		
ANOVA (between surveys)	NS		.01		NS			
direction	no change		contacts decreased		no change			

[a] NS = Not significant at .05 level.
Source: Community attitude surveys 1 and 2.

Table 32
SIGNIFICANCE OF CHANGES IN COMMUNITY ATTITUDES BY AGE AND RACE/ETHNICITY

	COMPOSITE VARIABLES														
	Fear of Crime			Opinions of Crime Trend			Security Effort			Acquaintance with Police			Police Use of Time		
GROUP	Study Areas														
	Cn	No	Sp	Cn	No	Sp	Cn	No	Sp	Cn	No	Sp	Cn	No	Sp
AGE															
16-19					.01							.05			
20-34				<.01	.01	<.01					<.01	.05			
35-49				.02	<.01		<.01								
50 & over		.03		.01	<.01	.01		.04	<.01						NA
RACE/ETHNICITY															
Black				<.01	.01										
Mexican-American															
White		.03	.01	<.01	<.01	<.01	.05					<.01			
ALL PERSONS		.03	.05	<.01	<.01	<.01					<.01	<.01			

Table 32 (continued)

	COMPOSITE VARIABLES											
	Rights of Police			Experience with Crime			Service Satis-faction			Police Initiated Contacts		
GROUP	Study Areas											
	Cn	No	Sp	Cn	No	Sp	Cn	No	Sp	Cn	No	Sp
AGE												
16-19												
20-34	.04				.04						.01	
35-49												
50 & over				.01	.03		.01					
RACE/ETHNICITY												
Black												.03
Mexican-American				.05							.03	
White					<.01			.01	<.01			
ALL PERSONS					.03	<.01	<.01	<.01			.01	

A blank means not significant at .05 level; NA = There were insufficient numbers of observations for the ANOVA test.
Cn = Control Area. No = No-FI Area. Sp = Special FI area.
Source: Community attitude surveys 1 and 2.

60

Table 33
MULTIPLE REGRESSION OF ATTITUDE VARIABLES ON
DEMOGRAPHIC, AREA, AND TIME VARIABLES

EQUATION	DEPENDENT VARIABLE	R^{2a}	INDEPENDENT VARIABLE SHOWING STRONGEST CORRELATIONS
1	Fear of Crime	.02	Sex
2	Opinions of Crime Trend	.04	Survey area
3	Security Efforts	.01	Survey area
4	Personal Acquaintance with Police	.05	Age
5	Police Use of Time	.04	Age
6	Rights of Police	.13	Age
7	Experience with Crime	.08	Age
8	Service Satisfaction with Calls for Service	.05	Survey time
9	Police Initiated Contacts	.11	Age

[a] The model assumed additive effects for each of these independent variables.
NOTE: The same set of six independent variables was used in each equation. These were: (1) age, (2) sex, (3) race (White or non-White), (4) survey time, (5) No-FI Area (yes or no), (6) Special FI Area (yes or no). With the exception of age, all variables were coded 0 or 1.

Table 34
SAN DIEGO POLICE DEPARTMENT COMPLAINT HISTORY

MONTH	FI-GENERATED COMPLAINTS	TOTAL COMPLAINTS	TOTAL DEPARTMENT FIELD INTERROGATIONS
Sept. '73	9	250	4057
Oct.	11	212	2401
Nov.	7	174	1837
Dec.	2	172	1948
Jan. '74	5	143	2174
Feb.	5	220	2342
March	10	184	5054
April	6	183	4903
May	10	207	4366
Total	65	1745	29082

FI-trained officers; (2) officers who were observed, exercised wide individual latitude with regard to initiating FI contacts; and (3) except for three specific unrelated incidents that were atypical, the approach, attitude, and demeanor of all officers observed in FI encounters were polite and straightforward. By far the most common approach was to address the subject, "Hi, how ya doin'?" It is probable that many subjects were not aware of being field interrogated.

(4.) Interviews with Field Interrogation Subjects

Twenty-eight individuals were interviewed; of these, 13 had been field interrogated by Control officers and 15 by Special FI officers. All the interviews were of male subjects. The age, sex, and race/ethnicity distributions of the individuals are shown in Table 35.

Table 35 reveals approximately the same distribution skew that was apparent in the age and race/ethnicity distribution of Field Interrogations reported by Control and Special FI officers, and is considered representative of the Field Interrogations observed.

Based on the responses given by FI subjects, Table 36 reveals there were differences in the subjects' reactions to Control and to Special FI officers. Subjects field interrogated by Special FI

61

officers responded more favorably to the encounter than did subjects field interrogated by Control officers.

When combining both officer groups, we find that 75 percent of the subjects agreed that the stop was legitimate. Seventy-nine percent of the subjects expressed the view that the officer had properly handled the interrogation.

By far the majority of the subjects (86 percent) indicated that the encounter would not or had not materially changed their attitude toward police or police stops. Therefore, in the majority of cases neither negative nor positive attitudes towards police were altered.

Only 14 percent of the respondents indicated that they would instruct a relative not to cooperate with the officer making the stop.

Table 35
AGE, SEX, AND RACE/ETHNICITY DISTRIBUTIONS OF INTERVIEWED
FIELD INTERROGATION SUBJECTS

JUVENILE				MALE				BLACK				MEXICAN-AMERICAN			
Control		Special FI		Control		Special FI		Control		Special FI		Control		Special FI	
(N)	(%)	(N)	(%)	(N)	(%)	(N)	(%)	(N)	(%)	(N)	(%)	(N)	(%)	(N)	(%)
7	53.9	10	66.9	13	100	15	100	6	46.2	7	46.7	3	23.1	3	20.1

Table 36
RESULTS OF INTERVIEWS WITH FIELD INTERROGATION SUBJECTS

	RESPONSES	
INTERVIEW QUESTIONS	Control Officer FI	Special FI Officer
Was the stop legitimate and/or do you think the officer has a right to stop you?		
Yes	8 (61.5)	13 (86.7)
No	3 (23.1)	2 (13.3)
Don't know	2 (15.4)	0 (.0)
Did the officer handle it properly?		
Yes	10 (76.9)	12 (80.0)
No	2 (15.4)	2 (13.3)
Don't know	1 (7.7)	1 (6.7)
How did you feel toward the officer?		
Positive	0 (.0)	9 (60.0)
Neutral	6 (46.1)	4 (26.6)
Negative	7 (53.9)	2 (13.3)
Did this incident change your attitude toward police?		
No	12 (92.3)	12 (80.0)
Yes	1 (7.7)	2 (13.3)
Don't know	0 (.0)	1 (6.7)
How would you instruct a relative to act if stopped by police?		
Avoid contact	4 (30.8)	3 (20.0)
Cooperate	4 (30.8)	7 (47.7)
Not to cooperate	3 (23.1)	1 (6.7)
Don't know	2 (15.4)	4 (26.6)

QUESTION 4: Do the benefits of Field Interrogations justify their cost to community relations and to patrol operations?

FINDINGS

(1.) *Field Interrogations were shown to have probable crime deterrent benefits. FI activities were also shown to contribute to patrol arrests. However, the benefits of reported FI data to crime investigations and to case clearances appeared to be limited by the current manual filing system used for FI reports.*

(2.) *The cost of FI practices to community relations is apparently minimal. Suspending or increasing Field Interrogations were shown to have little influence on public opinion. The use of FI practices is a traditional part of patrol operations in the city and is accepted as both an appropriate and properly performed police function by a vast majority of citizens, including those who were FI subjects. During the FI study there were no observed abuses of FI subjects, and no citizen complaints related to Field Interrogations were received from the study areas.*

(3.) *The average cost to patrol operations to conduct Field Interrogations in the Control and Special FI Areas was approximately 30 minutes of patrol time per beat, per day, and seems to be well justified by the probable benefits.*

SUMMARY OF ANALYSIS

The relative cost of FI practices to patrol operations was not directly evaluated during the study. The time spent in conducting and reporting Field Interrogations could conceivably be better used for a variety of other patrol officer-initiated activities such as public crime prevention education, traffic enforcements, or increased citizen service activities. None of these alternatives, or the many other possibilities, was directly evaluated. In reality, however, very little patrol time was used for Field Interrogations in the study areas. The average number of Field Interrogations conducted each day during the Experimental period was .9 per day in the Control Area and 1.7 per day in the Special FI Area.

Based on observation data, the average FI encounter (from the time of initial visual contact to final completion of the FI report and entry on the officer's daily report) was estimated to take 25 minutes. The approximate time spent on each element of a typical single-subject FI encounter was estimated:

ACTIVITY	MINUTES
Initial visual detection, to stop of subject	2
Questioning and observation of FI subject	15
FI report completion from notebook entries	5
FI entry on officer's daily report	3
Total	25

An average of approximately 22 minutes per day was spent on Field Interrogations in the Control Area, 42 minutes in the Special FI Area, and 0 minutes in the No-FI Area.

Of course, some time is also spent on contacts initiated by officer suspicion during which the officer's suspicions are allayed and no record is made. The exact proportion of these is not known, though the observers developed the impression that such contacts occur as frequently as those that lead to a report. Resolved contacts are of shorter duration and no recording time is needed. The additional time spent on such resolved contacts might have increased the total time per day spent on this class of activity by perhaps half an hour in the Control Area, and proportionately more in the Special FI Area.

In view of the relatively stable crime rates in the Control and Special FI Areas as compared to the significantly increased rates in the No-FI Area, the time costs—especially at the standard level in the Control Area—would seem to be justified.

The 20-minute daily average spread between the time spent to record Field Interrogations in the Control and in the Special FI Areas had no significant effect on the relative changes in the crime rates of the two areas. Although this experiment is not considered an adequate test of the effects of various levels of FI activity, it would appear that there may be a definite point of diminishing returns.

In summary, FI activities seem to be a justified use of patrol time, but the optimum levels of FI efforts were not determined in this evaluation and should be the subject of further study.

QUESTION 5: Is there a method for optimizing the benefits of Field Interrogations while minimizing the negative effects Field Interrogations have on police-community relations?

CONCLUSIONS AND RECOMMENDATIONS

(1.) *At the present time the two principal benefits of Field Interrogations are their probable deterrent effect on crimes and their contribution to arrests made by patrol officers. Potentially, the benefits of Field Interrogations might be expanded by increasing the use of FI data by investigators, through providing a computer-based FI file search system.*

(2.) *Although there was little evidence that FI activities influenced police-community relations in San Diego, there were some indications that the community might consider any increase in the currently low level of FI activity as an inappropriate use of patrol time. Pending further investigation, the current levels of activity should not be increased and FI quotas should not be established for patrol officers.*

Analysis of responses from the sample of FI subjects who were interviewed indicated that those subjects field interrogated by the Special FI-trained officers were more likely to react positively to the encounter experience than were subjects field interrogated by Control officers. In view of the above and the department's finding that the Special FI training differed from the regular academy training in only two respects (the use of videotape for self-analysis, and experiencing a Field Interrogation as a subject does), the department should re-examine the possibility of including some form of these two training elements in its academy program.

VI. AN EXAMINATION OF SOME ALTERNATIVE EXPLANATIONS OF THE EXPERIMENTAL FINDINGS

Because the authors and reviewers of this report were aware that the findings would be controversial, a special effort was made to identify and discuss factors that might have influenced the outcome of the experiment.

DATA MANIPULATION

There may be those who suspect that the San Diego Police Department somehow arranged its reporting or its police services to ensure that Field Interrogations would be found to be a significant crime deterrent. In theory, a dispatcher might ignore some calls for service, or patrol officers might make fewer arrests or simply spend more time in one area than another.

While in theory such a manipulation of crime data and police services is possible, the evidence from the San Diego study indicates that no such manipulation occurred.

First, the total numbers of patrol dispatches and arrests, as well as the ratios of arrests to dispatches, were higher in the No-FI Area than in the Control Area: the No-FI Area had 2,556 dispatches and 366 reported arrests, for a ratio of one arrest per 7.0 dispatches; the ratio in the Control Area was one arrest per 9.6 dispatches (277 reported arrests and 2,175 dispatches). There were no significant differences in the quality of arrests made in the study areas.

Second, evidence to counter any claim of police manipulation of crime reports comes from the community surveys, which showed that only the citizens in the No-FI Area reported a significant increase in opinion that crime was increasing during the period of the experiment. This confirmed the accuracy of the police-reported changes in crimes in the three areas, that the only area having a significant increase was the No-FI Area. Furthermore, there were no citizen complaints of unanswered calls for service, failures to file crime reports, or failures to make arrests.

Patrol presence was not measured during the study, but results of the recent Kansas City Preventive Patrol Experiment tend to cast serious doubts on the crime deterrence of routine preventive patrol.

In summary, no evidence could be found to support the theory of police manipulation of either crime reporting or services, while strong evidence was found to indicate that no such manipulation occurred.

FAILURE TO MAINTAIN THE FIELD INTERROGATION MORATORIUM IN THE NO-FI AREA

Although it is possible that Field Interrogations were conducted but not reported, the evidence indicates that this was not the case.

The FI project staff implemented, and System Development Corporation (SDC) monitored, a series of control activities that were designed to ensure that Field Interrogations were not conducted in the No-FI Area and, in general, to guarantee total project integrity:

- All department personnel were briefed on the project and its objectives prior to the start of the field phase.
- Monthly written project reminders and reports were sent to all administrative and commanding officers.

- All patrol personnel assigned to the Special FI and No-FI Areas received the special FI training and were fully aware of the project objectives and restrictions.
- Patrol captains, lieutenants, and sergeants were personally contacted frequently by the project staff, and were informed of the progress of the project and reminded of the moratorium in the No-FI Area.
- Patrol officers in all study areas were contacted in the field by the project staff.
- All FI forms were reviewed daily to detect any from the No-FI Area.
- All daily reports of officers assigned to the study areas were reviewed daily for any FI activities not reported on FI forms.

Another source of evidence comes from reports filed by patrol officers working in the No-FI Area, stating their observations relating to crime and crime-related problems when Field Interrogations were discontinued. In December 1973, the sergeant in charge of the officers working in the No-FI Area indicated that, because the officers were not allowed to make Field Interrogations, there appeared to be problems developing with juveniles. "The patrol officers are not able to control the juvenile gathering spots and as a result, problems of narcotics peddling, fights, and disorderly conduct are on the increase." Patrol officers in the No-FI Area frequently expressed concern that burglaries and thefts were getting out of control after Field Interrogations were stopped.

LARGE EFFECTS FROM SMALL NUMBERS—INADEQUATE SAMPLE SIZES

The practical limits of this field experiment dictated that only three patrol beats formed the study area and that the FI moratorium be limited to nine months. Although a rigorous selection process was employed to select representative and well-matched beats, it is possible that some unique set of unmeasured community characteristics or some short-lived crime phenomena may have influenced the results.

In the case of the FI experiment, there is evidence that the selected areas are reasonably well-matched and representative of the city of San Diego, and that the time period was of sufficient duration to identify the significant effects of FI activities there. The analysis of crime and arrest data focused on proportional changes in rates, rather than on absolute rates, as a means to adjust for any remaining differences among the selected areas.

The authors feel that in all probability an expanded study area or project duration, although desirable, would not materially have changed the results of the FI experiment in San Diego. The question whether or not similar experimental results would be obtained in other cities remains for other researchers to answer. However, two points should be carefully considered in any future comparison: (1) Field Interrogations are a traditional and well-accepted practice in San Diego; and (2) all San Diego police officers routinely receive extensive training in FI practice (which was augmented by special training for the experimental officer group). Therefore, this experiment was not a test of untrained versus trained officers, but rather of regularly trained versus more extensively trained officers.

ONLY UNIQUE LOCAL GROUPS WERE DETERRED BY FIELD INTERROGATIONS

It is possible that the population of potential criminal offenders that was deterred by police FI activity in the San Diego study areas might not be representative of such groups in other areas, and that therefore, the deterrent effects might not be typical of what could be expected in other areas.

This study indicated that some FI activity, as opposed to no FI activity, had a probable deterrent effect on reported crimes. The areas included in the study were typical (for San Diego), racially mixed, residential areas with a mix of single-family homes and apartments, small businesses, schools, and other public facilities. Although the potential offender populations of the areas were not identified, a majority of the FI subjects were male, non-White, and were not local residents; almost half were juveniles.

It seems probable that similar groups could be expected in similar areas of San Diego and perhaps elsewhere. While this study did not specifically address the question of which types of potential offenders were most influenced by FI activities, no evidence was found to indicate that unique groups existed in the study areas.

FIELD INTERROGATION ACTIVITIES MAY ONLY RESULT IN LOCAL AREA CRIME DISPLACEMENT

In theory, suspending Field Interrogations in one area may have caused offenders to shift their activity to that area. Similarly, resuming or increasing Field Interrogations may have caused offenders to shift their activities away from one area, to others. Thus, FI activities may not have affected the amount of crime, but merely its location.

Although all three study areas were in the same geographical area of San Diego, the areas were not contiguous. Moreover, no data were gathered for regions surrounding the study areas, some of which were outside the city of San Diego. Crime displacement, therefore, was not evaluated.

Given the mobility of all citizens, including potential crime offenders and FI subjects, some level of area displacement seems likely, and displacement effects should receive further study. Such a study would require not only detailed crime reports from surrounding areas, but also details on the levels and the nature of all patrol activity and specifically of arrests and Field Interrogations. Since the study of crime displacement was not an objective of this evaluation, the necessary data were not collected during the experiment, nor are they available for collection now. The data simply are not routinely maintained in the detail necessary for this analysis.

APPENDIX A: San Diego Police Academy Curriculum

SAN DIEGO POLICE ACADEMY CURRICULUM

*Contains material related to Field Interrogations.

BOOK III. TRAFFIC CONTROL

Animal Regulations	1
Citations: Mechanics & Psychology	4
Civil Disturbances	4
Commanding Officer Time	6
Criminal Justice System	6
Crowd Control	2
Driver Education I	8
Driver Education II	12
Drunk Driving	4
Municipal Ordinances	2
Traffic Accident Investigation	8
Traffic Control	4
Traffic Laws	6
Traffic Policies	2
Vehicle Pullovers*	3
Examination	3
	75

BOOK IV. LAW ENFORCEMENT COMMUNITY RELATIONS

Bill of Rights	2
Civil Liberties	4
Commanding Officer Time	9
Criminal Justice System	9
Methods of Arrest	4
General Public Relations	4
Graduation	2
Human Relations*	2
Interviews: Personal Relations*	4
Mental Illness	2
Press Relations	1
Race & Ethnic Group Relations*	16
Role Play Demonstration*	5
Role of Police in Society*	2
TV/Radio Orientation	1
Examination	3
	70

BOOK V. INTRODUCTION TO INVESTIGATIVE TECHNIQUES

Auto Theft	2
Collection, Preservation, & ID of Evidence	2
Commanding Officer Time	2
Crime Scene Recording	2
Criminal Investigation: Assaults	3
Criminal Investigation: Burglary	3
Criminal Investigation: Robbery	3
Criminal Law*	14
Criminal Justice System	2
Explosive Device Recognition	2
Field Interrogations*	6
Field Interviews*	2
Fingerprinting	4
Juvenile Law*	2

---

*Contains material related to Field Interrogations.

Juvenile Procedures*	6
Missing Persons	2
Narcotics & Dangerous Drugs	8
Preliminary Investigation	7
Rules of Evidence	5
Search Warrants	2
Sex Crimes	3
Fraud & Bunco Cases	2
Examination	3
	87

BOOK VI.   ARREST & CONTROL TECHNIQUES

Arrest & Control Techniques	6
Defensing Tactics	55
Transportation of Prisoners & Mentally III	2
Examination	2
	65

BOOK VII.   WEAPONRY

Firearms	29
Legal & Moral Aspects	4
Special Weapons	6

BOOK VIII.   EMERGENCY MEDICAL TRAINING

Emergency Medical Training	80

TOTAL CLASSROOM HOURS	607
TOTAL FIELD TRAINING HOURS	200
TOTAL ACADEMY HOURS	807

*Contains material related to Field Interrogations.

APPENDIX B: Community Attitude Survey

This appendix is comprised of expanded information concerning the two surveys of Community attitudes conducted as part of the San Diego Police Department/Police Foundation Field Interrogation Project. Results gleaned from the surveys that applied directly to the project analysis are reported in Chapter 5 of this report.

This appendix describes:

1. Sampling procedures employed to select the individual survey respondents.

2. Survey response rates and respondent/non-respondent characteristics. (Tables B-1 through B-4.)

3. A comparison of the distribution of demographic and socioeconomic characteristics of the respondents to the two surveys. (Table B-5.)

4. A catalog of the responses to each of the 68 questionnaire items. (Table B-6.)

5. Responses to some of the open-ended survey items. (Tables B-7 and B-8.)

A. SAMPLING PROCEDURE FOR SURVEY OF COMMUNITY ATTITUDES (1973)

The same sampling procedure was employed in each of the three areas included in the experiment. A probability sample was drawn from each area so that each housing unit had an approximately equal probability of being included in the sample and, for any included housing unit, each member 16 years or older had an equal chance of being chosen as respondent. With this procedure, unbiased estimates of household attitudes within a beat may be derived without the introduction of weights.

Since our response rate was expected to be about 65 percent and since we wished to obtain 167 (one-third of 500) completed interviews per area, a sample size 264 was drawn from each area. Each sample consisted of clusters of housing units that are geographically dispersed throughout the area. Each cluster comprised six consecutive housing units. This cluster size represented a compromise between budget constraints and the desirability of independence among sample observations.

In order to facilitate the computation of variance estimates and of confidence limits, we employed a replicated sampling design. In each area, the sample was composed of two independent sample-halves each of which was obtained in accordance with the same sampling procedure.

The sampling procedure for each sample-half involved two stages. The first was the selection of clusters of housing units and the second the selection of individual respondents from the housing units in the sample.

The sample design was rigid for it did not permit the interviewers any freedom in the selection either of the housing unit or of the respondent. No substitutions were permitted for an intended respondent who could not be reached after the required number of callbacks or who refused to be interviewed. These restrictions are necessary in order to maintain the scientific basis for making inferences about the population from the sample.

It was required that the person in the household who was selected to be interviewed be contacted three times, at varying times of the day and days of the week, before he be classified as non-respondent. Over ten percent of the work of each interviewer was verified. The verification process was carried out simultaneously with the field work so as to be able to identify and remove from the field as soon as possible any interviewer whose performance was inadequate.

As indicated above, in each area two half-samples were selected. The procedure for obtaining a half-sample involved the following two steps.*

1. Identification of the Clusters of Housing Units

The blocks of the area were ordered in serpentine fashion (i.e., geographically) and listed together with the numbers of housing units they contained. A column of cumulated housing units for these blocks was then recorded. The total number

---

*For further details see Survey Research, by Charles H. Backstrom and Gerald D. Hursh, Northwestern University Press, Illinois, 1963.

of housing units in the area was divided by the number of clusters of housing units in the half-sample; this number is called the skip interval. By means of a table or random numbers, a start number between 1 and the skip interval was selected. The block in which this number of cumulated housing units fell then contained the first cluster. The skip interval was added to this first number to obtain the next number, and so forth.

This procedure was repeated to identify the blocks in which these cumulated housing unit numbers fell. The next step was to locate the housing units within these blocks. This was done by setting up a procedure for selecting the initial housing unit of a block and by determining the direction along which housing units were to be counted until the designated cumulated housing unit number was reached. The cluster then consisted of the six consecutive housing units beginning with this unit.

The initial housing unit from which housing units in the block were to be counted was one of the four block corners (NE, NW, SE, SW) selected at random. The interviewer was directed to start counting housing units in a clockwise direction until the cluster to be included in the sample was reached.

2. Identification of the Person in the Household to be Interviewed

This was achieved by the use of a respondent-selection key. The key determined the respondent as a function of the number of eligible respondents in the housing unit and the number of eligible males. Alternative versions of the key were inserted in sequence into the questionnaires. These respondent-selection keys were designed so that each eligible member of a sample housing unit had approximately an equal chance of being selected for the interview.

The numbers of completed interviews were 162 in the Control Area, 208 in the No-FI Area, and 171 in the Special FI Area. Detailed characteristics of respondents and those who refused to respond may be found in Tables B-1 and B-2.

Table B-1. San Diego Community Attitude Survey 1973:
Characteristics of Respondents

	Control Area		No FI Area		Special FI Area		Totals	
	Number	Percent	Number	Percent	Number	Percent	Number	Percent
Sample Size *	245	100.0	251	100.0	239	100.0	735	100.0
Completions	162	66.1	208	82.9	171	71.5	541	73.6
Race *								
White	124	76.5	155	74.5	110	64.3	389	71.9
Black	22	13.6	12	5.8	21	12.3	55	10.2
Mexican-American	15	9.3	26	12.5	27	15.8	68	12.6
Other	1	.6	15	7.2	13	7.6	29	5.4
Sex **								
Male	70	43.2	84	40.4	78	45.6	232	42.9
Female	92	56.8	124	59.6	93	54.4	309	57.1
Age ***								
16-19	18	11.1	15	7.2	19	11.2	52	9.6
20-34	44	27.2	99	47.6	76	44.7	219	40.5
35-49	37	22.8	50	24.0	52	30.6	139	25.7
50+	63	38.9	44	21.3	23	13.5	130	24.0
Type Housing ***								
Own	126	77.8	141	67.8	151	88.3	418	77.3
Rent	36	22.2	67	32.2	20	11.7	123	22.7
Quality of Housing **								
Below Average	12	7.4	9	4.3	10	5.8	31	6.7
Average	123	75.9	157	75.4	142	83.0	422	78.0
Above Average	27	16.7	42	20.3	19	11.1	88	16.3

* Occupied housing units.

** Data based on observations by Survey Staff.

*** Data based on responses by subjects of survey.

Table B-2. San Diego Community Attitude Survey 1973: Characteristics of Refusals to Participate

	Control Area		No FI Area		Special FI Area		Totals	
	Number	Percent	Number	Percent	Number	Percent	Number	Percent
Sample Size *	245	100.0	251	100.0	239	100.0	735	100.0
Total Non-Respondents	83	33.9	43	17.1	68	28.4	194	26.4
No Contact Made	13	5.3	19	7.6	21	8.8	53	7.2
Refused to Participate **	70	28.6	24	9.6	47	19.7	141	19.2
Race								
White	60	85.7	17	70.8	34	72.3	111	78.7
Black	6	8.6	0	0	7	14.9	13	9.2
Mexican-American	4	5.7	4	16.7	4	8.5	12	8.5
Other	0	0	3	12.5	2	4.3	5	3.5
Sex								
Male	21	30.0	18	75.0	15	31.9	54	38.3
Female	49	70.0	6	25.0	32	68.1	87	61.7
Age								
16-19	0	0	1	4.2	1	2.1	2	1.4
20-34	14	20.0	9	37.5	14	29.8	37	26.2
35-49	23	32.8	5	20.8	22	46.8	60	42.5
50+	33	47.1	9	37.5	10	21.3	52	36.9
Type Housing								
Apartment	5	7.1	7	29.2	1	2.1	13	9.2
Home	65	92.9	17	70.8	46	97.9	128	90.8
Quality of Housing								
Below Average	2	2.8	2	8.3	2	4.3	6	4.2
Average	63	90.0	20	83.3	44	93.6	127	90.0
Above Average	5	7.2	2	8.3	1	2.1	8	5.8

* Occupied housing units.

** All data based on observations by Survey Staff.

The response rates for the three areas, measured as percent of occupied housing units in the sample for which interviews were completed, ranged from 66 percent to 83 percent. The overall response rate for all three areas was 74 percent.

The 26 percent that did not respond constituted 19 percent who refused to participate and 7 percent who could not be reached. In comparison with the respondents, those that refused to participate included larger proportions of females, home (rather than apartment) dwellers, and persons over 34 years old. Thus, one may reasonably conjecture that hostility to police was not a significant explanatory factor for non-response.

B. SAMPLING PROCEDURE FOR SURVEY OF COMMUNITY ATTITUDES (1974)

The design of the sample for the second survey was the same as that for the first, with approximately equal sample sizes in each area. The housing units of this sample were selected at the same time as were the housing units of the first survey. In each area the second sample consisted of two independent sample halves. Each of these consisted of clusters of six consecutive housing units adjacent (in clockwise direction) to the clusters of a sample half of the first survey.

It was decided not to interview the same household twice, for this could arouse hostility or otherwise contaminate response to the second survey. In order to avoid including the same household in both surveys, the sampling procedure required modification in two cases. This occurred when housing units of clusters of the two half-samples of the first survey were very close to each other. The rule was to skip over any housing units that had been included in the first survey, and then to continue in clockwise direction.

The selection of the person in the household to be interviewed was by means of a respondent-selection key. This procedure, which was employed in the first survey, is described above.

Callback and verification procedures were the same as those of the first survey. The numbers of completed interviews were 181 for the Control Area, 224 for the No-FI Area, and 202 for the Special FI Area. Detailed characteristics of respondents and those who refused to respond may be found in Tables B-3 and B-4.

Table B-3. San Diego Community Attitude Survey 1974:
Characteristics of Respondents

	Control Area		No FI Area		Special FI Area		Totals	
	Number	Percent	Number	Percent	Number	Percent	Number	Percent
Sample Size *	240	100.0	262	100.0	277	100.0	779	100.0
Completions	181	75.0	224	85.5	202	72.9	607	77.9
Race **								
White	133	73.5	159	71.0	137	67.8	429	70.7
Black	32	17.7	11	4.9	29	14.4	72	11.9
Mexican-American	12	6.6	32	14.3	29	14.4	73	12.0
Other	4	2.2	22	9.8	7	3.5	33	5.4
Sex **								
Male	76	42.0	102	45.5	96	47.5	274	45.1
Female	105	58.0	122	54.5	106	52.5	333	54.9
Age ***								
16-19	8	4.4	19	8.5	20	10.0	47	7.8
20-34	55	30.6	107	47.8	98	48.8	260	43.0
35-49	36	20.0	55	24.6	52	25.9	143	23.6
50+	81	45.0	43	19.2	31	15.4	155	25.6
Type Housing ***								
Own	145	81.5	152	68.2	177	88.1	474	78.7
Rent	33	18.5	71	31.8	24	11.9	128	21.3
Quality of Housing **								
Below Average	18	9.9	14	6.3	5	2.5	37	6.1
Average	142	78.5	188	83.9	125	61.9	455	75.0
Above Average	21	11.6	22	9.8	72	35.6	115	18.9

* Occupied housing units.
** Data based on observations by Survey Staff.
*** Data based on responses by subjects of survey.

Table B-4. San Diego Community Attitude Survey 1974:
Characteristics of Refusals to Participate

	Control Area		No FI Area		Special FI Area		Totals	
	Number	Percent	Number	Percent	Number	Percent	Number	Percent
Sample Size *	240	100.0	262	100.0	277	100.0	779	100.0
Total Non-Respondents	59	24.6	38	14.5	76	27.5	173	22.2
No Contact Made	41	17.1	13	5.0	37	13.4	91	11.7
Refused to Participate **	18	7.5	25	9.5	39	14.1	82	10.5
Race								
White	11	68.8	13	59.1	31	79.5	55	71.4
Black	2	12.5	4	18.2	4	10.3	10	13.0
Mexican-American	2	12.5	3	13.6	3	7.7	8	10.4
Other	1	6.2	2	9.1	1	2.6	4	5.2
Sex								
Male	6	33.3	14	60.9	11	28.2	31	38.8
Female	12	66.7	9	39.1	28	71.8	49	61.2
Age								
16-19	0	0	0	0	1	2.6	1	1.3
20-34	8	47.1	9	39.1	12	31.6	29	37.2
35-49	2	11.8	7	30.4	13	34.2	22	28.2
50+	7	41.2	7	30.4	12	31.6	26	33.3
Type Housing								
Apartment	2	13.3	8	33.3	1	2.6	9	11.5
Home	13	86.7	16	66.7	38	97.4	69	88.5
Quality of Housing								
Below Average	3	18.8	4	16.7	6	15.8	13	16.7
Average	13	81.2	20	83.3	29	76.3	62	79.5
Above Average	0	0	0	0	3	7.9	3	3.8

* Occupied housing units.

** All data based on observations by Survey Staff.

The response rate for the three areas, measured as percent of occupied housing units, ranged from 73 percent to 85 percent. The overall response rate was 78 percent. The 22 percent of non-respondents consisted of 10 percent who refused to participate and 12 percent who could not be reached. Differences between respondents and those who refused to participate were similar to those noted in the first survey. The latter group contained a larger proportion of females, a larger proportion of older people and a larger proportion of home (rather than apartment) dwellers. The two groups had almost identical racial compositions. (Respondents were 71 percent White, 12 percent Black, 13 percent Mexican-American; those that refused to participate were 72 percent White, 13 percent Black, and 9 percent Mexican-American.)

Both surveys were conducted under the direction of Dr. Oscar J. Kaplan, Director of the Center for Survey Research of San Diego State University.

C. <u>DEMOGRAPHIC AND SOCIOECONOMIC CHARACTERISTICS OF SURVEY RESPONDENTS</u>

The following pages contain Table B-5, a series of tabular data which provide the demographic and socioeconomic characteristics of the respondents. This table compares the distribution of demographic and socioeconomic characteristics of the respondents of the two surveys, separately for each area. The questions covered are those in Part II of the survey instrument. Data was printed only for those that responded; those that answered 'Don't Know' or for whom there was no response recorded are omitted. Each page is concerned with a single question. Results are shown separately, by area. For each area, results are presented in two arrays. The first array gives actual numbers: the first row refers to the first survey, and the second row to the second survey. The second array gives percentages for the first and second surveys; these are shown on the upper and lower lines, respectively. The percentage figures omit the decimal point. For example, on the first page of the Table, the first entry of the upper line (first survey) in the <u>row percent</u> array is printed '362' and should be read as 36.2 percent. Results of the Chi Square test of significance of the difference in frequency distributions between the first and second surveys are presented for each question, by area.

CONTINGENCY TABLE

								D.F. =	6	CHI-SQUARE =	6.68343
COL NO OF CHILDREN 69
ROW BEAT 1/SRVY 1&2 251 — PROBABILITY OF CHI-SQUARE = 0.35112

CONTROL:

	1.0	2.0	3.0	4.0	5.0	6.0	7.0	TOTAL
11	25	22	10	4	3	3	2	69
12	27	24	7	7	2	0	0	67
TOTAL	52	46	17	11	5	3	2	136

ROW PERCENT

	1.0	2.0	3.0	4.0	5.0	6.0	7.0	TOTAL
11	362	319	145	58	43	43	29	1000
12	403	358	104	104	30	0	0	1000
TOTAL	382	338	125	81	37	22	15	1000

CONTINGENCY TABLE

COL NO OF CHILDREN 69 — D.F. = 6 — CHI-SQUARE = 4.61066
ROW BEAT 2/SRVY 1&2 251 — PROBABILITY OF CHI-SQUARE = 0.59463

No FI:

	1.0	2.0	3.0	4.0	5.0	6.0	7.0	TOTAL
11	42	41	23	6	10	1	1	124
12	43	55	27	8	4	1	2	140
TOTAL	85	96	50	14	14	2	3	264

ROW PERCENT

	1.0	2.0	3.0	4.0	5.0	6.0	7.0	TOTAL
11	339	331	185	48	81	8	8	1000
12	307	393	193	57	29	7	14	1000
TOTAL	322	364	189	53	53	8	11	1000

CONTINGENCY TABLE

COL NO OF CHILDREN 69 — D.F. = 6 — CHI-SQUARE = 4.28657
ROW BEAT 3/SRVY 1&2 251 — PROBABILITY OF CHI-SQUARE = 0.63796

SPEC. FI:

	1.0	2.0	3.0	4.0	5.0	6.0	7.0	TOTAL
11	38	37	20	13	8	6	0	122
12	41	39	21	19	6	3	2	131
TOTAL	79	76	41	32	14	9	2	253

ROW PERCENT

	1.0	2.0	3.0	4.0	5.0	6.0	7.0	TOTAL
11	311	303	164	107	66	49	0	1000
12	313	298	160	145	46	23	15	1000
TOTAL	312	300	162	126	55	36	8	1000

* 1973 Survey results are shown in the upper line; 1974 Survey results are shown in the lower line.

Response percentages are shown in tenths of a percent (NNN) and should be read as NN.N%.

COMMUNITY CRIME SURVEY - TIME 1 and 2*

CONTINGENCY TABLE

COL OWN OR RENT 70 — D.F. = 1 — CHI-SQUARE = 0.71108
ROW BEAT 1/SRVY 1&2 251 — PROBABILITY OF CHI-SQUARE = 0.39909

CONTROL:

	1.0	2.0	TOTAL
11	126	36	162
12	145	33	178
TOTAL	271	69	340

ROW PERCENT

	1.0	2.0	TOTAL
11	778	222	1000
12	815	185	1000
TOTAL	797	203	1000

CONTINGENCY TABLE

COL OWN OR RENT 70 — D.F. = 1 — CHI-SQUARE = 0.00658
ROW BEAT 2/SRVY 1&2 251 — PROBABILITY OF CHI-SQUARE = 0.93537

No FI:

	1.0	2.0	TOTAL
11	141	67	208
12	152	71	223
TOTAL	293	138	431

ROW PERCENT

	1.0	2.0	TOTAL
11	678	322	1000
12	682	318	1000
TOTAL	680	320	1000

CONTINGENCY TABLE

COL OWN OR RENT 70 — D.F. = 1 — CHI-SQUARE = 0.00497
ROW BEAT 3/SRVY 1&2 251 — PROBABILITY OF CHI-SQUARE = 0.94382

SPEC. FI:

	1.0	2.0	TOTAL
11	151	20	171
12	177	24	201
TOTAL	328	44	372

ROW PERCENT

	1.0	2.0	TOTAL
11	883	117	1000
12	881	119	1000
TOTAL	882	118	1000

* 1973 Survey results are shown in the upper line; 1974 Survey results are shown in the lower line.

Response percentages are shown in tenths of a percent (NNN) and should be read as NN.N%.

COMMUNITY CRIME SURVEY - TIME 1 and 2*

CONTINGENCY TABLE

COL OCCUPATION 71   D.F. = 8   CHI-SQUARE = 16.58925
ROW BEAT 1/SRVY 1&2 251   PROBABILITY OF CHI-SQUARE = 0.03468

CONTROL:

	1.0	2.0	3.0	4.0	5.0	6.0	7.0	8.0	9.0	TOTAL
11	20	29	20	7	3	16	25	40	1	161
12	12	21	38	18	4	10	30	43	4	180
TOTAL	32	50	58	25	7	26	55	83	5	341

ROW PERCENT

	1.0	2.0	3.0	4.0	5.0	6.0	7.0	8.0	9.0	TOTAL
11	124	180	124	43	19	99	155	248	6	1000
12	67	117	211	100	22	56	167	239	22	1000
TOTAL	94	147	170	73	21	76	161	243	15	1000

CONTINGENCY TABLE

COL OCCUPATION 71   D.F. = 8   CHI-SQUARE = 7.97975
ROW BEAT 2/SRVY 1&2 251   PROBABILITY OF CHI-SQUARE = 0.43545

No FI:

	1.0	2.0	3.0	4.0	5.0	6.0	7.0	8.0	9.0	TOTAL
11	26	26	39	16	8	9	14	65	4	207
12	35	27	33	22	4	20	12	65	5	223
TOTAL	61	53	72	38	12	29	26	130	9	430

ROW PERCENT

	1.0	2.0	3.0	4.0	5.0	6.0	7.0	8.0	9.0	TOTAL
11	126	126	188	77	39	43	68	314	19	1000
12	157	121	148	99	18	90	54	291	22	1000
TOTAL	142	123	167	88	28	67	60	302	21	1000

CONTINGENCY TABLE

COL OCCUPATION 71   D.F. = 8   CHI-SQUARE = 2.90989
ROW BEAT 3/SRVY 1&2 251   PROBABILITY OF CHI-SQUARE = 0.93988

SPEC. FI:

	1.0	2.0	3.0	4.0	5.0	6.0	7.0	8.0	9.0	TOTAL
11	15	16	43	20	3	11	5	52	6	171
12	23	22	38	21	4	14	6	59	9	196
TOTAL	38	38	81	41	7	25	11	111	15	367

ROW PERCENT

	1.0	2.0	3.0	4.0	5.0	6.0	7.0	8.0	9.0	TOTAL
11	88	94	251	117	18	64	29	304	35	1000
12	117	112	194	107	20	71	31	301	46	1000
TOTAL	104	104	221	112	19	68	30	302	41	1000

* 1973 Survey results are shown in the upper line; 1974 Survey results are shown in the lower line.

* Response percentages are shown in tenths of a percent (NNN) and should be read as NN.N%.

COMMUNITY CRIME SURVEY - TIME 1 and 2*

CONTINGENCY TABLE

COL AGE 72   D.F. = 3   CHI-SQUARE = 6.40213
ROW BEAT 1/SRVY 1&2 251   PROBABILITY OF CHI-SQUARE = 0.09360

CONTROL:

	1.0	2.0	3.0	4.0	TOTAL
11	18	44	37	63	162
12	8	55	36	81	180
TOTAL	26	99	73	144	342

ROW PERCENT

	1.0	2.0	3.0	4.0	TOTAL
11	111	272	228	389	1000
12	44	306	200	450	1000
TOTAL	76	289	213	421	1000

CONTINGENCY TABLE

COL AGE 72   D.F. = 3   CHI-SQUARE = 0.44515
ROW BEAT 2/SRVY 1&2 251   PROBABILITY OF CHI-SQUARE = 0.93077

No FI:

	1.0	2.0	3.0	4.0	TOTAL
11	15	98	50	44	207
12	19	107	55	43	224
TOTAL	34	205	105	87	431

ROW PERCENT

	1.0	2.0	3.0	4.0	TOTAL
11	72	473	242	213	1000
12	85	478	246	192	1000
TOTAL	79	476	244	202	1000

CONTINGENCY TABLE

COL AGE 72   D.F. = 3   CHI-SQUARE = 1.41171
ROW BEAT 3/SRVY 1&2 251   PROBABILITY OF CHI-SQUARE = 0.70279

SPEC. FI:

	1.0	2.0	3.0	4.0	TOTAL
11	19	76	52	23	170
12	20	98	52	31	201
TOTAL	39	174	104	54	371

ROW PERCENT

	1.0	2.0	3.0	4.0	TOTAL
11	112	447	306	135	1000
12	100	488	259	154	1000
TOTAL	105	469	280	146	1000

* 1973 Survey results are shown in the upper line; 1974 Survey results are shown in the lower line.

Response percentages are shown in tenths of a percent (NNN) and should be read as NN.N%.

CONTINGENCY TABLE

COL EDUCATION 73 D.F. = 8 CHI-SQUARE = 2.3821?
ROW BEAT 1/SRVY 1&2 251 PROBABILITY OF CHI-SQUARE = 0.96700

CONTROL:

	1.0	2.0	3.0	4.0	5.0	6.0	7.0	8.0	9.0	TOTAL
11	8	9	26	59	3	5	42	6	3	161
12	7	10	38	67	4	4	43	5	2	180
TOTAL	15	19	64	126	7	9	85	11	5	341

ROW PERCENT

	1.0	2.0	3.0	4.0	5.0	6.0	7.0	8.0	9.0	TOTAL
11	50	56	161	366	19	31	261	37	19	1000
12	39	56	211	372	22	22	239	28	11	1000
TOTAL	44	56	188	370	21	26	249	32	15	1000

CONTINGENCY TABLE

COL EDUCATION 73 D.F. = 8 CHI-SQUARE = 14.39195
ROW BEAT 2/SRVY 1&2 251 PROBABILITY OF CHI-SQUARE = 0.07210

No FI:

	1.0	2.0	3.0	4.0	5.0	6.0	7.0	8.0	9.0	TOTAL
11	9	7	40	85	3	9	42	7	6	208
12	3	6	40	74	6	26	50	11	8	224
TOTAL	12	13	80	159	9	35	92	18	14	432

ROW PERCENT

	1.0	2.0	3.0	4.0	5.0	6.0	7.0	8.0	9.0	TOTAL
11	43	34	192	409	14	43	202	34	29	1000
12	13	27	179	330	27	116	223	49	36	1000
TOTAL	28	30	185	368	21	81	213	42	32	1000

CONTINGENCY TABLE

COL EDUCATION 73 D.F. = 8 CHI-SQUARE = 4.38350
ROW BEAT 3/SRVY 1&2 251 PROBABILITY OF CHI-SQUARE = 0.82097

SPEC. FI:

	1.0	2.0	3.0	4.0	5.0	6.0	7.0	8.0	9.0	TOTAL
11	5	6	40	63	1	8	39	7	2	171
12	8	9	46	63	5	7	53	7	3	201
TOTAL	13	15	86	126	6	15	92	14	5	372

ROW PERCENT

	1.0	2.0	3.0	4.0	5.0	6.0	7.0	8.0	9.0	TOTAL
11	29	35	234	368	6	47	228	41	12	1000
12	40	45	229	313	25	35	264	35	15	1000
TOTAL	35	40	231	339	16	40	247	38	13	1000

* 1973 Survey results are shown in the upper line; 1974 Survey results are shown in the lower line.

Response percentages are shown in tenths of a percent (NNN) and should be read as NN.N%.

COMMUNITY CRIME SURVEY - TIME 1 AND 2*

CONTINGENCY TABLE

COL MARITAL STATUS 74 D.F. = 4 CHI-SQUARE = 2.40459
ROW BEAT 1/SRVY 1&2 251 PROBABILITY OF CHI-SQUARE = 0.66180

CONTROL:

	1.0	2.0	3.0	4.0	5.0	TOTAL
11	108	2	15	10	27	162
12	122	2	18	17	22	181
TOTAL	230	4	33	27	49	343

ROW PERCENT

	1.0	2.0	3.0	4.0	5.0	TOTAL
11	667	12	93	62	167	1000
12	674	11	99	94	122	1000
TOTAL	671	12	96	79	143	1000

CONTINGENCY TABLE

COL MARITAL STATUS 74 D.F. = 4 CHI-SQUARE = 5.40033
ROW BEAT 2/SRVY 1&2 251 PROBABILITY OF CHI-SQUARE = 0.24863

No FI:

	1.0	2.0	3.0	4.0	5.0	TOTAL
11	160	0	16	10	22	208
12	179	1	9	6	29	224
TOTAL	339	1	25	16	51	432

ROW PERCENT

	1.0	2.0	3.0	4.0	5.0	TOTAL
11	769	0	77	48	106	1000
12	799	4	40	27	129	1000
TOTAL	785	2	58	37	118	1000

CONTINGENCY TABLE

COL MARITAL STATUS 74 D.F. = 4 CHI-SQUARE = 0.42224
ROW BEAT 3/SRVY 1&2 251 PROBABILITY OF CHI-SQUARE = 0.98062

SPEC. FI:

	1.0	2.0	3.0	4.0	5.0	TOTAL
11	129	2	15	4	21	171
12	155	2	17	3	25	202
TOTAL	284	4	32	7	46	373

ROW PERCENT

	1.0	2.0	3.0	4.0	5.0	TOTAL
11	754	12	88	23	123	1000
12	767	10	84	15	124	1000
TOTAL	761	11	86	19	123	1000

* 1973 Survey results are shown in the upper line; 1974 Survey results are shown in the lower line.

Response percentages are shown in tenths of a percent (NNN) and should be read as NN.N%.

COMMUNITY CRIME SURVEY - TIME 1 AND 2*

CONTROL:

CONTINGENCY TABLE				
COL WAGE EARNER M/F 75			D.F. = 1 CHI-SQUARE = 0.32911	
ROW BEAT 1/SRVY 1&2 251			PROBABILITY OF CHI-SQUARE = 0.56619	
	1.0	2.0	TOTAL	
11	127	33	160	
12	139	42	181	
TOTAL	286	75	341	

ROW PERCENT			
	1.0	2.0	TOTAL
11	794	206	1000
12	768	232	1000
TOTAL	780	220	1000

No FI:

CONTINGENCY TABLE				
COL WAGE EARNER M/F 75			D.F. = 1 CHI-SQUARE = 0.07375	
ROW BEAT 2/SRVY 1&2 251			PROBABILITY OF CHI-SQUARE = 0.78596	
	1.0	2.0	TOTAL	
11	184	24	208	
12	200	24	224	
TOTAL	384	48	432	

ROW PERCENT			
	1.0	2.0	TOTAL
11	885	115	1000
12	893	107	1000
TOTAL	889	111	1000

SPEC. FI:

CONTINGENCY TABLE				
COL WAGE EARNER M/F 75			D.F. = 1 CHI-SQUARE = 0.25401	
ROW BEAT 3/SRVY 1&2 251			PROBABILITY OF CHI-SQUARE = 0.61426	
	1.0	2.0	TOTAL	
11	155	16	171	
12	179	22	201	
TOTAL	334	38	372	

ROW PERCENT			
	1.0	2.0	TOTAL
11	906	94	1000
12	891	109	1000
TOTAL	898	102	1000

* 1973 Survey results are shown in the upper line; 1974 Survey results are shown in the lower line.

Response percentages are shown in tenths of a percent (NNN) and should be read as NN.N%.

COMMUNITY CRIME SURVEY - TIME 1 AND 2*

CONTROL:

CONTINGENCY TABLE							
COL SOURCE OF NEWS 76					D.F. = 5 CHI-SQUARE = 58.88121		
ROW BEAT 1/SRVY 1&2 251					PROBABILITY OF CHI-SQUARE = 0.00000		
	1.0	2.0	3.0	4.0	5.0	6.0	TOTAL
11	61	18	40	8	31	1	159
12	61	10	9	2	96	0	178
TOTAL	122	28	49	10	127	1	337

ROW PERCENT						
	1.0	2.0	3.0	4.0	5.0	6.0	TOTAL
11	384	113	252	50	195	6	1000
12	343	56	51	11	539	0	1000
TOTAL	362	83	145	30	377	3	1000

No FI:

CONTINGENCY TABLE							
COL SOURCE OF NEWS 76					D.F. = 5 CHI-SQUARE = 3.01599		
ROW BEAT 2/SRVY 1&2 251					PROBABILITY OF CHI-SQUARE = 0.69752		
	1.0	2.0	3.0	4.0	5.0	6.0	TOTAL
11	88	12	26	6	71	2	205
12	93	13	24	7	86	0	223
TOTAL	181	25	50	13	157	2	428

ROW PERCENT						
	1.0	2.0	3.0	4.0	5.0	6.0	TOTAL
11	429	59	127	29	346	10	1000
12	417	58	108	31	386	0	1000
TOTAL	423	58	117	30	367	5	1000

SPEC. FI:

CONTINGENCY TABLE							
COL SOURCE OF NEWS 76					D.F. = 5 CHI-SQUARE = 0.67401		
ROW BEAT 3/SRVY 1&2 251					PROBABILITY OF CHI-SQUARE = 0.98436		
	1.0	2.0	3.0	4.0	5.0	6.0	TOTAL
11	67	12	21	6	64	1	171
12	77	14	23	5	79	2	200
TOTAL	144	26	44	11	143	3	371

ROW PERCENT						
	1.0	2.0	3.0	4.0	5.0	6.0	TOTAL
11	392	70	123	35	374	6	1000
12	385	70	115	25	395	10	1000
TOTAL	388	70	119	30	385	8	1000

* 1973 Survey results are shown in the upper line; 1974 Survey results are shown in the lower line.

Response percentages are shown in tenths of a percent (NNN) and should be read as NN.N%.

CONTINGENCY TABLE

CONTROL:

COL FAMILY INCOME 77   D.F. = 8   CHI-SQUARE = 12.86279
ROW BEAT 1/SRVY 1&2 251   PROBABILITY OF CHI-SQUARE = 0.11666

	1.0	2.0	3.0	4.0	5.0	6.0	7.0	8.0	9.0	TOTAL
11	8	8	7	10	6	24	43	16	5	127
12	6	15	12	3	11	21	32	20	10	130
TOTAL	14	23	19	13	17	45	75	36	15	257

ROW PERCENT

	1.0	2.0	3.0	4.0	5.0	6.0	7.0	8.0	9.0	TOTAL
11	63	63	55	79	47	189	339	126	39	1000
12	46	115	92	23	85	162	246	154	77	1000
TOTAL	54	89	74	51	66	175	292	140	58	1000

CONTINGENCY TABLE

No FI:

COL FAMILY INCOME 77   D.F. = 8   CHI-SQUARE = 4.26254
ROW BEAT 2/SRVY 1&2 251   PROBABILITY OF CHI-SQUARE = 0.83269

	1.0	2.0	3.0	4.0	5.0	6.0	7.0	8.0	9.0	TOTAL
11	4	13	10	13	15	25	61	23	13	177
12	2	16	13	7	15	23	72	28	13	189
TOTAL	6	29	23	20	30	48	133	51	26	366

ROW PERCENT

	1.0	2.0	3.0	4.0	5.0	6.0	7.0	8.0	9.0	TOTAL
11	23	73	56	73	85	141	345	130	73	1000
12	11	85	69	37	79	122	381	148	69	1000
TOTAL	16	79	63	55	82	131	363	139	71	1000

CONTINGENCY TABLE

SPEC. FI:

COL FAMILY INCOME 77   D.F. = 8   CHI-SQUARE = 16.67473
ROW BEAT 3/SRVY 1&2 251   PROBABILITY OF CHI-SQUARE = 0.03368

	1.0	2.0	3.0	4.0	5.0	6.0	7.0	8.0	9.0	TOTAL
11	5	4	11	7	7	30	68	14	5	151
12	4	2	7	9	5	21	52	30	15	145
TOTAL	9	6	18	16	12	51	120	44	20	296

ROW PERCENT

	1.0	2.0	3.0	4.0	5.0	6.0	7.0	8.0	9.0	TOTAL
11	33	26	73	46	46	199	450	93	33	1000
12	28	14	48	62	34	145	359	207	103	1000
TOTAL	30	20	61	54	41	172	405	149	68	1000

*1973 Survey results are shown in the upper line; 1974 Survey results are shown in the lower line.

Response percentages are shown in tenths of a percent (NNN) and should be read as NN.N%.

CONTINGENCY TABLE

CONTROL:

COL SEX 78   D.F. = 1   CHI-SQUARE = 0.05201
ROW BEAT 1/SRVY 1&2 251   PROBABILITY OF CHI-SQUARE = 0.81960

	1.0	2.0	TOTAL
11	70	92	162
12	76	105	181
TOTAL	146	197	343

ROW PERCENT

	1.0	2.0	TOTAL
11	432	568	1000
12	420	580	1000
TOTAL	426	574	1000

CONTINGENCY TABLE

No FI:

COL SEX 78   D.F. = 1   CHI-SQUARE = 1.16675
ROW BEAT 2/SRVY 1&2 251   PROBABILITY OF CHI-SQUARE = 0.28007

	1.0	2.0	TOTAL
11	84	124	208
12	102	122	224
TOTAL	186	246	432

ROW PERCENT

	1.0	2.0	TOTAL
11	404	596	1000
12	455	545	1000
TOTAL	431	569	1000

CONTINGENCY TABLE

SPEC. FI:

COL SEX 78   D.F. = 1   CHI-SQUARE = 0.13553
ROW BEAT 3/SRVY 1&2 251   PROBABILITY OF CHI-SQUARE = 0.71277

	1.0	2.0	TOTAL
11	78	93	171
12	96	106	202
TOTAL	174	199	373

ROW PERCENT

	1.0	2.0	TOTAL
11	456	544	1000
12	475	525	1000
TOTAL	466	534	1000

*1973 Survey results are shown in the upper line; 1974 Survey results are shown in the lower line.

Response percentages are shown in tenths of a percent (NNN) and should be read as NN.N%.

COMMUNITY CRIME SURVEY - TIME 1 AND 2*

CONTINGENCY TABLE

CONTROL:

| COL RACE | | 79 | | | | D.F. = 4 | CHI-SQUARE = 3.25769 |
| ROW BEAT 1/SRVY 1&2 | 251 | | | | | PROBABILITY OF CHI-SQUARE = 0.51566 |

	1.0	2.0	3.0	4.0	5.0	TOTAL
11	22	124	15	1	0	162
12	32	133	12	4	0	181
TOTAL	54	257	27	5	0	343

ROW PERCENT

	1.0	2.0	3.0	4.0	5.0	TOTAL
11	136	765	93	6	0	1000
12	177	735	66	22	0	1000
TOTAL	157	749	79	15	0	1000

CONTINGENCY TABLE

No FI:

| COL RACE | | 79 | | | | D.F. = 4 | CHI-SQUARE = 5.05426 |
| ROW BEAT 2/SRVY 1&2 | 251 | | | | | PROBABILITY OF CHI-SQUARE = 0.28178 |

	1.0	2.0	3.0	4.0	5.0	TOTAL
11	12	155	26	11	4	208
12	11	159	32	21	1	224
TOTAL	23	314	58	32	5	432

ROW PERCENT

	1.0	2.0	3.0	4.0	5.0	TOTAL
11	58	745	125	53	19	1000
12	49	710	143	94	4	1000
TOTAL	53	727	134	74	12	1000

CONTINGENCY TABLE

SPEC. FI:

| COL RACE | | 79 | | | | D.F. = 4 | CHI-SQUARE = 3.75178 |
| ROW BEAT 3/SRVY 1&2 | 251 | | | | | PROBABILITY OF CHI-SQUARE = 0.44064 |

	1.0	2.0	3.0	4.0	5.0	TOTAL
11	21	110	27	7	6	171
12	29	137	29	3	4	202
TOTAL	50	247	56	10	10	373

ROW PERCENT

	1.0	2.0	3.0	4.0	5.0	TOTAL
11	123	643	158	41	35	1000
12	144	678	144	15	20	1000
TOTAL	134	662	150	27	27	1000

*1973 Survey results are shown in the upper line; 1974 Survey results are shown in the lower line.

Response percentages are shown in tenths of a percent (NNN) and should be read as NN.N%.

COMMUNITY CRIME SURVEY - TIME 1 AND 2*

CONTINGENCY TABLE

CONTROL:

| COL HOUSING RATING | | 80 | | D.F. = 2 | CHI-SQUARE = 2.26655 |
| ROW BEAT 1/SRVY 1&2 | 251 | | | PROBABILITY OF CHI-SQUARE = 0.32198 |

	1.0	2.0	3.0	TOTAL
11	27	123	12	162
12	21	142	18	181
TOTAL	48	265	30	343

ROW PERCENT

	1.0	2.0	3.0	TOTAL
11	167	759	74	1000
12	116	785	99	1000
TOTAL	140	773	87	1000

CONTINGENCY TABLE

No FI:

| COL HOUSING RATING | | 80 | | D.F. = 2 | CHI-SQUARE = 9.65806 |
| ROW BEAT 2/SRVY 1&2 | 251 | | | PROBABILITY OF CHI-SQUARE = 0.00799 |

	1.0	2.0	3.0	TOTAL
11	42	156	9	207
12	22	188	14	224
TOTAL	64	344	23	431

ROW PERCENT

	1.0	2.0	3.0	TOTAL
11	203	754	43	1000
12	98	839	63	1000
TOTAL	148	798	53	1000

CONTINGENCY TABLE

SPEC. FI:

| COL HOUSING RATING | | 80 | | D.F. = 2 | CHI-SQUARE = 31.25609 |
| ROW BEAT 3/SRVY 1&2 | 251 | | | PROBABILITY OF CHI-SQUARE = 0.00000 |

	1.0	2.0	3.0	TOTAL
11	19	142	10	171
12	72	125	5	202
TOTAL	91	267	15	373

ROW PERCENT

	1.0	2.0	3.0	TOTAL
11	111	830	58	1000
12	356	619	25	1000
TOTAL	244	716	40	1000

*1973 Survey results are shown in the upper line; 1974 Survey results are shown in the lower line.

Response percentages are shown in tenths of a percent (NNN) and should be read as NN.N%.

D. SURVEY RESULTS

Table A-6 presents the results of our two surveys of community attitudes. The Table consists of 68 pages, one for each attitudinal question. On each page the exact wording of the question, as it appears in the survey instrument, is given. Results are presented separately for each area. The column headed "Number" gives the number of individuals who responded to the question; those that answered Don't Know ('0') are excluded from this total. It is for this reason that response numbers are not equal for all questions. Entries in the remaining columns are percentages. These percentages were computed after exclusion of those that did not know or did not respond. For each area, the distributions of responses in percentages for the first and second surveys are shown in the first and second lines, respectively. Decimal points were omitted in printing these percentages. Thus, the first percentage on the first line of the first page of the Table which is written '167', should be read as 16.7 percent. The third line gives the differences in percentage response between the first and second surveys.

SAN DIEGO POLICE DEPARTMENT FI PROJECT - COMMUNITY ATTITUDINAL SURVEY RESULTS
RESPONSE PERCENTAGES BY BEAT

> **1.** How many persons age 16 or over live in this household? (1) 1;
> (2) 2; (3) 3: (4) 4; (5) 5; (6) 6; (7) 7; (8) 8; (9) 9 or more

	RESPONSES: NUMBER	1	2	3	4	5 NN.N%*	6	7	8	9
CONTROL: BEAT 1										
SURVEY 1	162	167	593	130	86	25	0	0	0	0
SURVEY 2	181	188	619	105	61	22	6	0	0	0
DIFFERENCE		-21	-26	25	25	3	-6	0	0	0
No FI: BEAT 2										
SURVEY 1	208	163	673	125	38	0	0	0	0	0
SURVEY 2	224	94	661	143	63	31	9	0	0	0
DIFFERENCE		69	12	-18	-25	-31	-9	0	0	0
SPECIAL FI: BEAT 3										
SURVEY 1	171	70	643	193	70	12	6	0	6	0
SURVEY 2	202	89	663	188	50	10	0	0	0	0
DIFFERENCE		-19	-20	5	20	2	6	0	6	0

* Response Percentages are shown in tenths of a percent (NNN) and should be read as NN.N%.

SAN DIEGO POLICE DEPARTMENT FI PROJECT - COMMUNITY ATTITUDINAL SURVEY RESULTS
RESPONSE PERCENTAGES BY BEAT

> **2.** How long have you lived in this house or apartment? (1) Less than
> 6 months; (2) 6 months to 1 year; (3) 1 year to 2 years; (4) 2 years
> to 4 years; (5) 4 years or more.

	RESPONSES: NUMBER	1	2	3	4	5 NN.N%*	6	7	8	9
CONTROL: BEAT 1										
SURVEY 1	162	80	93	99	123	605				
SURVEY 2	181	110	66	61	83	680				
DIFFERENCE		-30	27	38	40	-75				
No FI: BEAT 2										
SURVEY 1	208	159	154	163	139	385				
SURVEY 2	223	108	179	135	121	457				
DIFFERENCE		51	-25	28	18	-72				
SPECIAL FI: BEAT 3										
SURVEY 1	171	111	82	175	170	462				
SURVEY 2	202	144	94	153	243	366				
DIFFERENCE		-33	-12	22	-73	96				

* Response Percentages are shown in tenths of a percent (NNN) and should be read as NN.N%.

3. About how long have you lived in this neighborhood? (SHOW MAP OF CENSUS TRACT BOUNDARIES.) (1) Less than 6 months; (2) 6 months to 1 year; (3) 1 year to 2 years; (4) 2 years to 4 years; (5) 4 years or more.

	RESPONSES: NUMBER	1	2	3	4	5 NN.N%*	6	7	8	9
CONTROL: **BEAT 1**										
SURVEY 1	162	68	74	68	130	660				
SURVEY 2	181	61	61	88	61	729				
DIFFERENCE		7	13	-20	69	-69				
No FI: **BEAT 2**										
SURVEY 1	208	154	120	130	144	452				
SURVEY 2	223	103	139	108	135	516				
DIFFERENCE		51	-19	22	9	-64				
SPECIAL FI: **BEAT 3**										
SURVEY 1	171	94	82	158	170	497				
SURVEY 2	202	134	84	139	228	416				
DIFFERENCE		-40	-2	19	-58	81				

* Response Percentages are shown in tenths of a percent (NNN) and should be read as NN.N%.

AN DIEGO POLICE DEPARTMENT FI PROJECT - COMMUNITY ATTITUDINAL SURVEY RESULTS
RESPONSE PERCENTAGES BY BEAT

4. Do you now work or attend school in this neighborhood? (1) yes; (2) No, work or school outside of area; (3) Don't work or go to school; (4) Unemployed.

	RESPONSES: NUMBER	1	2	3	4	5 NN.N%*	6	7	8	9
CONTROL: **BEAT 1**										
SURVEY 1	161	124	540	267	68					
SURVEY 2	181	77	497	376	50					
DIFFERENCE		47	43	-109	18					
No FI: **BEAT 2**										
SURVEY 1	208	38	558	361	43					
SURVEY 2	224	54	607	268	71					
DIFFERENCE		-16	-49	93	-28					
SPECIAL FI **BEAT 3**										
SURVEY 1	171	70	579	281	70					
SURVEY 2	202	124	500	347	30					
DIFFERENCE		-54	79	-66	40					

* Response Percentages are shown in tenths of a percent (NNN) and should be read as NN.N%.

> 5. The next group of questions will ask how much chance you think
> there is of different kinds of crime happening in this neigh-
> borhood. For example, how much chance do you think there is
> that you could be robbed or beaten up on the street during the
> day: (1) Very likely; (2) Somewhat likely; (3) Somewhat unlikely;
> (4) Very unlikely; (0) Don't know.

		RESPONSES: NUMBER	1	2	3	4 NN.N%*	5	6	7	8	9
CONTROL:	BEAT 1										
	SURVEY 1	155	129	110	148	613					
	SURVEY 2	174	109	178	236	477					
	DIFFERENCE		20	-68	-88	136					
No FI:	BEAT 2										
	SURVEY 1	194	67	108	216	608					
	SURVEY 2	216	157	199	213	431					
	DIFFERENCE		-90	-91	3	177					
SPECIAL FI:	BEAT 3										
	SURVEY 1	167	138	168	228	467					
	SURVEY 2	191	120	136	120	623					
	DIFFERENCE		18	32	108	-156					

* Response Percentages are shown in tenths of a percent (NNN) and should be read as NN.N%.

> 6. How much chance do you think there is that you could be robbed or
> beaten up on the street during the night in this neighborhood?
> (1) Very likely; (2) Somewhat likely; (3) Somewhat unlikely;
> (4) Very unlikely; (0) Don't know.

		RESPONSES: NUMBER	1	2	3	4 NN.N%*	5	6	7	8	9
CONTROL:	BEAT 1										
	SURVEY 1	153	235	268	150	346					
	SURVEY 2	170	253	282	253	212					
	DIFFERENCE		-18	-14	-103	134					
No FI:	BEAT 2										
	SURVEY 1	194	201	278	232	289					
	SURVEY 2	219	329	306	196	169					
	DIFFERENCE		-128	-28	36	120					
SPECIAL FI:	BEAT 3										
	SURVEY 1	166	229	295	211	265					
	SURVEY 2	186	269	258	204	269					
	DIFFERENCE		-40	37	7	-4					

* Response Percentages are shown in tenths of a percent (NNN) and should be read as NN.N%.

7. How much chance do you think there is that your home could be broken into while you are away during the day? (1) Very likely; (2) Somewhat likely; (3) Somewhat unlikely; (4) Very unlikely; (0) Don't know.

	RESPONSES: NUMBER	1	2	3	4	5 NN.N%*	6	7	8	9
CONTROL: BEAT 1										
SURVEY 1	154	396	221	162	221					
SURVEY 2	177	345	249	169	237					
DIFFERENCE		51	-28	-7	-16					
No FI: BEAT 2										
SURVEY 1	203	360	300	202	138					
SURVEY 2	219	374	301	128	196					
DIFFERENCE		-14	-1	74	-58					
SPECIAL FI: BEAT 3										
SURVEY 1	163	399	288	141	172					
SURVEY 2	196	393	179	163	265					
DIFFERENCE		6	109	-22	-93					

* Response Percentages are shown in tenths of a percent (NNN) and should be read as NN.N%.

8. How much chance do you think there is that your home could be broken into while you are away during the night? (1) Very likely; (2) Somewhat likely; (3) Somewhat unlikely; (4) Very unlikely; (0) Don't know.

	RESPONSES: NUMBER	1	2	3	4	5 NN.N%*	6	7	8	9
CONTROL: BEAT 1										
SURVEY 1	158	449	241	120	190					
SURVEY 2	174	397	218	201	184					
DIFFERENCE		52	23	-81	6					
No FI: BEAT 2										
SURVEY 1	201	488	299	114	100					
SURVEY 2	220	518	255	105	123					
DIFFERENCE		-30	44	9	-23					
SPECIAL FI: BEAT 3										
SURVEY 1	164	561	238	116	85					
SURVEY 2	196	464	204	168	163					
DIFFERENCE		97	34	-52	-78					

* Response Percentages are shown in tenths of a percent (NNN) and should be read as NN.N%.

9. In general then, would you say that your neighborhood is (1) Very
safe; (2) Moderately safe; (3) Slightly safe; (4) Slightly dangerous;
(5) Moderately dangerous; (6) Very dangerous; (0) Don't know.

	RESPONSES: NUMBER	1	2	3	4	5	6	7	8	9
					NN.N%*					
CONTROL: BEAT 1										
SURVEY 1	155	258	406	213	65	32	26			
SURVEY 2	177	175	514	113	113	51	34			
DIFFERENCE		83	-108	100	-48	-19	-8			
No FI: BEAT 2										
SURVEY 1	198	111	566	141	86	86	10			
SURVEY 2	222	99	545	140	113	90	14			
DIFFERENCE		12	21	1	-27	-4	-4			
SPECIAL FI: BEAT 3										
SURVEY 1	169	118	444	183	160	83	12			
SURVEY 2	193	130	477	166	140	73	16			
DIFFERENCE		-12	-33	17	20	10	-4			

* Response Percentages are shown in tenths of a percent (NNN) and should be read as NN.N%.

SAN DIEGO POLICE DEPARTMENT FI PROJECT - COMMUNITY ATTITUDINAL SURVEY RESULTS
RESPONSE PERCENTAGES BY BEAT

10. Comparing this neighborhood with other neighborhoods in the City
of San Diego, would you say that this neighborhood is: (1) Much
safer; (2) A little safer; (3) About the same; (4) A little more
dangerous; or (5) Much more dangerous; (0) Don't know.

	RESPONSES: NUMBER	1	2	3	4	5	6	7	8	9
					NN.N%*					
CONTROL: BEAT 1										
SURVEY 1	152	414	197	270	79	39				
SURVEY 2	171	152	351	368	99	29				
DIFFERENCE		262	-154	-98	-20	10				
No FI: BEAT 2										
SURVEY 1	179	229	324	352	67	28				
SURVEY 2	205	200	263	400	117	20				
DIFFERENCE		29	61	-48	-50	8				
SPECIAL FI: BEAT 3										
SURVEY 1	159	220	340	321	107	13				
SURVEY 2	180	161	294	378	150	17				
DIFFERENCE		59	46	-57	-43	-4				

* Response Percentages are shown in tenths of a percent (NNN) and should be read as NN.N%.

11. Of the crimes that occur in this neighborhood, how many would
    you say are committed by the people who live here: (1) Most
    by people who live here; (2) Half and half; (3) Most by outsiders;
    (4) No crime in neighborhood; (0) Don't know.

		RESPONSES: NUMBER	1	2	3	4	5	6	7	8	9
						NN.N%*					
CONTROL:	BEAT 1										
	SURVEY 1	119	218	134	387	261					
	SURVEY 2	139	317	158	360	165					
	DIFFERENCE		-99	-24	27	96					
No FI:	BEAT 2										
	SURVEY 1	168	274	262	351	113					
	SURVEY 2	188	457	165	261	117					
	DIFFERENCE		-183	97	90	-4					
SPECIAL FI:	BEAT 3										
	SURVEY 1	144	278	243	326	153					
	SURVEY 2	135	311	230	356	104					
	DIFFERENCE		-33	13	-30	49					

* Response Percentages are shown in tenths of a percent (NNN) and should be read as NN.N%.

12. What types of people do you think commit most of the crime in
    this neighborhood? DO NOT READ ALTERNATIVES. (1) Young whites;
    (2) Young blacks; (3) Young Mexican-Americans; (4) Young people
    in general; (5) Whites; (6) Blacks; (7) Mexican-Americans;
    (8) Drug users; (9) Other:

		RESPONSES: NUMBER	1	2	3	4	5	6	7	8	9
						NN.N%*					
CONTROL:	BEAT 1										
	SURVEY 1	95	0	63	0	611	0	53	11	147	116
	SURVEY 2	105	10	105	10	610	0	86	0	38	143
	DIFFERENCE		-10	-42	-10	1	0	-33	11	109	-27
No FI:	BEAT 2										
	SURVEY 1	139	0	22	7	748	7	36	0	122	58
	SURVEY 2	161	0	25	12	752	6	50	31	75	50
	DIFFERENCE		0	-3	-5	-4	1	-14	-31	47	8
SPECIAL FI:	BEAT 3										
	SURVEY 1	114	18	53	0	675	9	26	18	96	105
	SURVEY 2	110	9	27	18	636	0	45	18	36	209
	DIFFERENCE		9	26	-18	39	9	-19	0	60	-104

* Response Percentages are shown in tenths of a percent (NNN) and should be read as NN.N%.

13. Think now about violent crime in this neighborhood. I mean attacks on people (like shootings, stabbings, and rapes). Would you say that in the past year, as compared to previous years, things have been: (1) Little or no violent crime in this neighborhood; (2) Getting better; (3) Staying about the same; (4) Getting worse; (0) Don't know.

		RESPONSES: NUMBER	1	2	3	4	5	6	7	8	9
							NN.N%*				
CONTROL:	BEAT 1										
	SURVEY 1	137	292	44	445	219					
	SURVEY 2	154	636	39	175	149					
	DIFFERENCE		-344	5	270	70					
No FI:	BEAT 2										
	SURVEY 1	180	622	78	211	89					
	SURVEY 2	182	269	82	352	297					
	DIFFERENCE		353	-4	-141	-208					
SPECIAL FI:	BEAT 3										
	SURVEY 1	149	577	47	208	168					
	SURVEY 2	190	779	47	105	68					
	DIFFERENCE		-202	0	103	100					

* Response Percentages are shown in tenths of a percent (NNN) and should be read as NN.N%.

14. Think now about nonviolent crime in this neighborhood. I mean crime involving property (like burglary, auto theft, and vandalism). Would you say that during the past year, as compared to previous years, things have been: (1) Little or no nonviolent crime in this area; (2) Getting better; (3) Staying about the same; (4) Getting worse; (0) Don't know.

		RESPONSES: NUMBER	1	2	3	4	5	6	7	8	9
							NN.N%*				
CONTROL:	BEAT 1										
	SURVEY 1	137	117	58	416	409					
	SURVEY 2	172	163	93	430	314					
	DIFFERENCE		-46	-35	-14	95					
No FI:	BEAT 2										
	SURVEY 1	174	190	149	391	270					
	SURVEY 2	183	109	82	372	437					
	DIFFERENCE		81	67	19	-167					
SPECIAL FI:	BEAT 3										
	SURVEY 1	158	177	82	335	405					
	SURVEY 2	186	242	97	339	323					
	DIFFERENCE		-65	-15	-4	82					

* Response Percentages are shown in tenths of a percent (NNN) and should be read as NN.N%.

15. Within the last 12 months, have you done anything to protect
your home such as adding extra locks or bars, or installing
timer lights, burglar alarms, or other protection devices?
(1) Yes; (2) No.

		RESPONSES: NUMBER	1	2	3	4	5 NN.N%*	6	7	8	9
CONTROL:	BEAT 1										
	SURVEY 1	162	370	630							
	SURVEY 2	181	320	680							
	DIFFERENCE		50	-50							
No FI:	BEAT 2										
	SURVEY 1	208	438	563							
	SURVEY 2	224	460	540							
	DIFFERENCE		-22	23							
SPECIAL FI:	BEAT 3										
	SURVEY 1	171	421	579							
	SURVEY 2	202	327	673							
	DIFFERENCE		94	-94							

* Response Percentages are shown in tenths of a percent (NNN) and should be read as NN.N%.

16. Within the last 12 months, have you done any of the following
to protect yourself against crime: Obtained a dog, hired a
private security patrol, got a gun or other weapon, avoided
going out at night, or done anything else because you were
fearful of your personal safety? (1) Yes; (2) No.

		RESPONSES: NUMBER	1	2	3	4	5 NN.N%*	6	7	8	9
CONTROL:	BEAT 1										
	SURVEY 1	162	358	642							
	SURVEY 2	181	271	729							
	DIFFERENCE		87	-87							
No FI:	BEAT 2										
	SURVEY 1	208	370	630							
	SURVEY 2	224	366	634							
	DIFFERENCE		4	-4							
SPECIAL FI:	BEAT 3										
	SURVEY 1	171	380	620							
	SURVEY 2	202	208	792							
	DIFFERENCE		172	-172							

* Response Percentages are shown in tenths of a percent (NNN) and should be read as NN.N%.

17. Now here are some questions about the San Diego Police. In
    general, when it comes to fighting crime in the entire city,
    do you think that they are doing: (1) A good job; (2) A fair
    job; (3) A poor job; (0) Don't know.

		NUMBER	1	2	3	4	5	6	7	8	9
							NN.N%*				
CONTROL:	BEAT 1										
	SURVEY 1	150	580	327	93						
	SURVEY 2	169	609	325	65						
	DIFFERENCE		-29	2	28						
No FI:	BEAT 2										
	SURVEY 1	187	604	316	80						
	SURVEY 2	208	577	341	82						
	DIFFERENCE		27	-25	-2						
SPECIAL FI:	BEAT 3										
	SURVEY 1	161	565	354	81						
	SURVEY 2	166	488	343	169						
	DIFFERENCE		77	11	-88						

* Response Percentages are shown in tenths of a percent (NNN) and should be read as NN.N%.

SAN DIEGO POLICE DEPARTMENT FI PROJECT - COMMUNITY ATTITUDINAL SURVEY RESULTS
RESPONSE PERCENTAGES BY BEAT

18. What about the police in this neighborhood? When it comes to
    fighting crime in this neighborhood, do you think that they
    are doing: (1) A good job; (2) A fair job; (3) A poor job;
    (0) Don t know.

		NUMBER	1	2	3	4	5	6	7	8	9
							NN.N%*				
CONTROL:	BEAT 1										
	SURVEY 1	133	714	195	90						
	SURVEY 2	157	592	312	96						
	DIFFERENCE		122	-117	-6						
No FI:	BEAT 2										
	SURVEY 1	190	537	316	147						
	SURVEY 2	213	432	315	254						
	DIFFERENCE		105	1	-107						
SPECIAL FI:	BEAT 3										
	SURVEY 1	154	558	312	130						
	SURVEY 2	154	455	318	227						
	DIFFERENCE		103	-6	-97						

* Response Percentages are shown in tenths of a percent (NNN) and should be read as NN.N%.

19. Is there anything in particular about police service in this
neighborhood that you like? (DO NOT READ ALTERNATIVES. IF
MORE THAN ONE ANSWER GIVEN, PROBE FOR MOST IMPORTANT.)
(1) Come quickly when called; (2) Are polite and friendly;
(3) Frequent patrols--adequate number of police; (4) Do a good
job of solving crimes; (5) Do a good job of keeping public
informed; (6) Participate in community activities; (7) Provide
ambulance and other emergency service; (8) Nothing in particular;
(9) Other answers--specify

		RESPONSES: NUMBER	1	2	3	4	5 NN.N%*	6	7	8	9
CONTROL:	BEAT 1										
	SURVEY 1	160	119	75	200	25	0	6	6	569	0
	SURVEY 2	181	155	55	193	0	11	0	11	569	6
	DIFFERENCE		-36	20	7	25	-11	6	-5	0	-6
No FI:	BEAT 2										
	SURVEY 1	208	96	48	168	24	19	0	10	635	0
	SURVEY 2	224	94	67	125	9	13	0	0	679	13
	DIFFERENCE		2	-19	43	15	6	0	10	-44	-13
SPECIAL FI:	BEAT 3										
	SURVEY 1	171	70	58	228	18	0	18	0	608	0
	SURVEY 2	201	50	40	234	15	0	0	5	632	25
	DIFFERENCE		20	18	-6	3	0	18	-5	-24	-25

* Response Percentages are shown in tenths of a percent (NNN) and should be read as NN.N%.

20. Is there anything in particular about police service in this
neighborhood that you don't like? (DO NOT READ ALTERNATIVES.
IF MORE THAN ONE ANSWER GIVEN, PROBE FOR MOST IMPORTANT.)
(1) Police are unfriendly; (2) Police don't care about this
neighborhood; (3) Police aren't patrolling enough--more police
needed; (4) Police are slow in answering calls; (5) Police are
unduly suspicious about people in neighborhood; (6) Police are
discourteous, improperly handle or abuse suspects; (7) Traffic
control is inadequate; (8) No complaints about police service;
(9) Other answers--specify

		RESPONSES: NUMBER	1	2	3	4	5 NN.N%*	6	7	8	9
CONTROL:	BEAT 1										
	SURVEY 1	162	12	12	86	49	12	56	12	741	1º
	SURVEY 2	181	11	17	138	77	17	0	6	702	33
	DIFFERENCE		1	-5	-52	-28	-5	56	6	39	-14
No FI:	BEAT 2										
	SURVEY 1	208	0	10	226	125	24	19	10	558	29
	SURVEY 2	223	18	22	256	152	9	13	4	516	9
	DIFFERENCE		-18	-12	-30	-27	15	6	6	42	20
SPECIAL FI:	BEAT 3										
	SURVEY 1	171	12	12	181	82	23	29	18	608	35
	SURVEY 2	202	0	5	129	109	45	20	15	639	40
	DIFFERENCE		12	7	52	-27	-22	9	3	-31	-5

* Response Percentages are shown in tenths of a percent (NNN) and should be read as NN.N%.

```
21. In the last 12 months, have you noticed any change in the way
    the police operate in this neighborhood?  (1) Yes, What _____
    _____
    (2) No; (0) Don't know.
```

		RESPONSES: NUMBER	1	2	3	4	5 NN.N%*	6	7	8	9
CONTROL:	BEAT 1										
	SURVEY 1	144	229	771							
	SURVEY 2	177	158	842							
	DIFFERENCE		71	-71							
No FI:	BEAT 2										
	SURVEY 1	192	151	849							
	SURVEY 2	214	206	794							
	DIFFERENCE		-55	55							
SPECIAL FI:	BEAT 3										
	SURVEY 1	163	337	663							
	SURVEY 2	162	191	809							
	DIFFERENCE		146	-146							

* Response Percentages are shown in tenths of a percent (NNN) and should be read as NN.N%.

```
22. About how often do you see officers in this neighborhood?
    (1) More than once a day; (2) About once a day; (3) Several
    times a week; (4) Once a week; (5) Once or twice a month;
    (6) Less than once a month; (7) Never or almost never;
    (0) Don't know.
```

		RESPONSES: NUMBER	1	2	3	4	5 NN.N%*	6	7	8	9
CONTROL:	BEAT 1										
	SURVEY 1	158	222	158	158	127	114	57	165		
	SURVEY 2	166	145	193	199	145	151	30	139		
	DIFFERENCE		77	-35	-41	-18	-37	27	26		
No FI:	BEAT 2										
	SURVEY 1	201	209	149	184	144	60	80	174		
	SURVEY 2	221	104	195	181	131	190	68	131		
	DIFFERENCE		105	-46	3	13	-130	12	43		
SPECIAL FI:	BEAT 3										
	SURVEY 1	168	268	179	173	131	161	30	60		
	SURVEY 2	193	223	204	109	88	78	21	218		
	DIFFERENCE		45	-85	64	43	83	9	-158		

* Response Percentages are shown in tenths of a percent (NNN) and should be read as NN.N%.

23. How would you say that the police and the people in this
neighborhood get along? (1) Very good; (2) Fairly good;
(3) Fairly bad; (4) Very bad; (0) Don't know.

		RESPONSES: NUMBER	1	2	3	4	5	6	7	8	9
					NN.N%*						
CONTROL:	BEAT 1										
	SURVEY 1	126	683	294	8	16					
	SURVEY 2	154	552	403	39	6					
	DIFFERENCE		131	-109	-31	10					
No FI:	BEAT 2										
	SURVEY 1	173	543	387	58	12					
	SURVEY 2	179	363	603	34	0					
	DIFFERENCE		180	-216	24	12					
SPECIAL FI:	BEAT 3										
	SURVEY 1	146	425	486	62	27					
	SURVEY 2	140	464	471	29	36					
	DIFFERENCE		-39	15	33	-9					

* Response Percentages are shown in tenths of a percent (NNN) and should be read as NN.N%.

24. Do you think that the police arrive fast enough when people
call for help? (1) Always; (2) Usually; (3) Sometimes;
(4) Never; (0) Don't know.

		RESPONSES: NUMBER	1	2	3	4	5	6	7	8	9
					NN.N%*						
CONTROL:	BEAT 1										
	SURVEY 1	122	311	270	123	295					
	SURVEY 2	142	352	296	190	162					
	DIFFERENCE		-41	-26	-67	133					
No FI:	BEAT 2										
	SURVEY 1	170	241	376	224	159					
	SURVEY 2	184	141	321	332	207					
	DIFFERENCE		100	55	-108	-48					
SPECIAL FI:	BEAT 3										
	SURVEY 1	155	187	329	342	142					
	SURVEY 2	148	108	291	216	385					
	DIFFERENCE		79	38	126	-243					

* Response Percentages are shown in tenths of a percent (NNN) and should be read as NN.N%.

> 25. How do you feel about the number of police officers in this
>   neighborhood? Does this neighborhood: (1) Need a lot more
>   officers; (2) Need a few more; (3) Have about the right
>   number; (4) Have too many officers; (0) Don't know.

		RESPONSES: NUMBER	1	2	3	4	5 NN.N%*	6	7	8	9
CONTROL:	BEAT 1										
	SURVEY 1	139	79	259	633	29				
	SURVEY 2	151	132	371	464	33				
	DIFFERENCE		-53	-112	169	-4				
No FI:	BEAT 2										
	SURVEY 1	185	108	503	389	0				
	SURVEY 2	194	175	510	294	21				
	DIFFERENCE		-67	-7	95	-21				
SPECIAL FI:	BEAT 3										
	SURVEY 1	156	103	391	462	45				
	SURVEY 2	161	56	478	441	25				
	DIFFERENCE		47	-87	21	20				

*Response Percentages are shown in tenths of a percent (NNN) and should be read as NN.N%.

> 26. Do you have a good friend or relative who is a police officer?
>   (1) Yes; (2) No.

		RESPONSES: NUMBER	1	2	3	4	5 NN.N%*	6	7	8	9
CONTROL:	BEAT 1										
	SURVEY 1	162	315	685						
	SURVEY 2	181	293	707						
	DIFFERENCE		22	-22						
No FI:	BEAT 2										
	SURVEY 1	208	317	683						
	SURVEY 2	224	344	656						
	DIFFERENCE		-27	27						
SPECIAL FI:	BEAT 3										
	SURVEY 1	171	392	608						
	SURVEY 2	200	235	765						
	DIFFERENCE		157	-157						

*Response Percentages are shown in tenths of a percent (NNN) and should be read as NN.N%.

27. Do you know the name of a police officer in this neighborhood?
    (1) Yes; (2) No.

		RESPONSES: NUMBER	1	2	3	4	5 NN.N%*	6	7	8	9
CONTROL:	BEAT 1										
	SURVEY 1	162	167	833							
	SURVEY 2	181	122	878							
	DIFFERENCE		45	-45							
No FI:	BEAT 2										
	SURVEY 1	208	53	947							
	SURVEY 2	224	67	933							
	DIFFERENCE		-14	14							
SPECIAL FI:	BEAT 3										
	SURVEY 1	171	88	912							
	SURVEY 2	200	45	955							
	DIFFERENCE		43	-43							

*Response Percentages are shown in tenths of a percent (NNN) and should be read as NN.N%.

SAN DIEGO POLICE DEPARTMENT FI PROJECT - COMMUNITY ATTITUDINAL SURVEY RESULTS
RESPONSE PERCENTAGES BY BEAT

28. Have you ever had a friendly or informal talk with a police
    officer? (1) Yes; (2) No.

		RESPONSES: NUMBER	1	2	3	4	5 NN.N%*	6	7	8	9
CONTROL:	BEAT 1										
	SURVEY 1	162	685	315							
	SURVEY 2	181	674	326							
	DIFFERENCE		11	-11							
No FI:	BEAT 2										
	SURVEY 1	208	639	361							
	SURVEY 2	224	679	321							
	DIFFERENCE		-40	40							
SPECIAL FI:	BEAT 3										
	SURVEY 1	171	678	322							
	SURVEY 2	202	604	396							
	DIFFERENCE		74	-74							

* Response Percentages are shown in tenths of a percent (NNN) and should be read as NN.N%.

29. I am going to read you several types of police activity in
your neighborhood and ask if you think they are spending the
proper amount of time on them. For example, patrolling in
cars, are they spending:(1) Too much time; (2) About the right
amount of time: (3) Too little time; (0) Don't know.

		RESPONSES: NUMBER	1	2	3	4	5 NN.N%*	6	7	8	9
CONTROL:	BEAT 1										
	SURVEY 1	131	61	672	267						
	SURVEY 2	147	48	544	408						
	DIFFERENCE		13	128	-141						
No FI:	BEAT 2										
	SURVEY 1	173	29	503	468						
	SURVEY 2	202	40	416	545						
	DIFFERENCE		-11	87	-77						
SPECIAL FI:	BEAT 3										
	SURVEY 1	153	52	529	418						
	SURVEY 2	125	96	488	416						
	DIFFERENCE		-44	41	2						

* Response Percentages are shown in tenths of a percent (NNN) and should be read as NN.N%.

30. Controlling traffic, are they spending:(1) Too much time;
(2) About the right amount of time; (3) Too little time;
(0) Don't know.

		RESPONSES: NUMBER	1	2	3	4	5 NN.N%*	6	7	8	9
CONTROL:	BEAT 1										
	SURVEY 1	126	40	706	254						
	SURVEY 2	131	84	702	214						
	DIFFERENCE		-44	4	40						
No FI:	BEAT 2										
	SURVEY 1	158	38	696	266						
	SURVEY 2	210	38	681	281						
	DIFFERENCE		0	15	-15						
SPECIAL FI:	BEAT 3										
	SURVEY 1	140	50	636	314						
	SURVEY 2	120	108	617	275						
	DIFFERENCE		-58	19	39						

* Response Percentages are shown in tenths of a percent (NNN) and should be read as NN.N%.

31. Investigating known crimes, are they spending:(1) Too much
time; (2) About the right amount of time; (3) Too little
time; (0) Don't know.

	RESPONSES:	1	2	3	4	5	6	7	8	9
	NUMBER					NN.N%*				
CONTROL: BEAT 1										
SURVEY 1	88	45	636	318						
SURVEY 2	104	0	673	327						
DIFFERENCE		45	-37	-9						
No FI: BEAT 2										
SURVEY 1	114	9	614	377						
SURVEY 2	181	11	564	425						
DIFFERENCE		-2	50	-48						
SPECIAL FI: BEAT 3										
SURVEY 1	98	20	582	398						
SURVEY 2	93	22	527	452						
DIFFERENCE		-2	55	-54						

* Response Percentages are shown in tenths of a percent (NNN) and should be read as NN.N%.

32. Assisting people in emergencies, are they spending:(1) Too
much time; (2) About the right amount of time; (3) Too
little time; (0) Don't know.

	RESPONSES:	1	2	3	4	5	6	7	8	9
	NUMBER					NN.N%*				
CONTROL: BEAT 1										
SURVEY 1	120	0	808	192						
SURVEY 2	136	0	875	125						
DIFFERENCE		0	-67	67						
No FI: BEAT 2										
SURVEY 1	151	7	834	159						
SURVEY 2	187	0	775	225						
DIFFERENCE		7	59	-66						
SPECIAL FI: BEAT 3										
SURVEY 1	139	7	827	165						
SURVEY 2	118	17	771	212						
DIFFERENCE		-10	56	-47						

* Response Percentages are shown in tenths of a percent (NNN) and should be read as NN.N%.

33. Helping settle family quarrels, are they spending:(1) Too
    much time; (2) About the right amount of time; (3) Too
    little time; (0) Don't know.

	RESPONSES:	1	2	3	4	5	6	7	8	9
	NUMBER					NN.N%*				
CONTROL: BEAT 1										
SURVEY 1	62	65	742	194						
SURVEY 2	77	91	792	117						
DIFFERENCE		-26	-50	77						
No FI: BEAT 2										
SURVEY 1	87	161	667	172						
SURVEY 2	109	92	697	211						
DIFFERENCE		69	-30	-39						
SPECIAL FI: BEAT 3										
SURVEY 1	75	93	693	213						
SURVEY 2	55	91	636	273						
DIFFERENCE		2	57	-60						

* Response Percentages are shown in tenths of a percent (NNN) and should be read as NN.N%.

34. Getting to know juveniles, are they spending:(1) Too much
    time; (2) About the right amount of time; (3) Too little
    time; (0) Don't know.

	RESPONSES:	1	2	3	4	5	6	7	8	9
	NUMBER					NN.N%*				
CONTROL: BEAT 1										
SURVEY 1	96	21	458	521						
SURVEY 2	114	18	447	535						
DIFFERENCE		3	11	-14						
No FI: BEAT 2										
SURVEY 1	133	38	398	564						
SURVEY 2	159	25	447	528						
DIFFERENCE		13	-49	36						
SPECIAL FI: BEAT 3										
SURVEY 1	119	17	437	546						
SURVEY 2	103	68	476	456						
DIFFERENCE		-51	-39	90						

* Response Percentages are shown in tenths of a percent (NNN) and should be read as NN.N%.

35. Questioning and searching suspicious persons, are they
spending:(1) Too much time; (2) About the right amount
of time; (3) Too little time; (0) Don't know.

		RESPONSES: NUMBER	1	2	3	4	5	6	7	8	9
							NN.N%*				
CONTROL:	BEAT 1										
	SURVEY 1	103	204	689	107						
	SURVEY 2	111	216	622	162						
	DIFFERENCE		-12	67	-55						
No FI:	BEAT 2										
	SURVEY 1	121	165	579	256						
	SURVEY 2	161	174	534	292						
	DIFFERENCE		-9	45	-36						
SPECIAL FI:	BEAT 3										
	SURVEY 1	107	234	542	224						
	SURVEY 2	90	444	378	178						
	DIFFERENCE		-210	164	46						

* Response Percentages are shown in tenths of a percent (NNN) and should be read as NN.N%.

36. Speaking to groups about crime prevention, are they
spending:(1) Too much time; (2) About the right amount
of time; (3) Too little time; (0) Don't know.

		RESPONSES: NUMBER	1	2	3	4	5	6	7	8	9
							NN.N%*				
CONTROL:	BEAT 1										
	SURVEY 1	103	19	524	456						
	SURVEY 2	115	17	565	417						
	DIFFERENCE		2	-41	39						
No FI:	BEAT 2										
	SURVEY 1	128	8	570	422						
	SURVEY 2	160	13	544	444						
	DIFFERENCE		-5	26	-22						
SPECIAL FI:	BEAT 3										
	SURVEY 1	104	29	577	394						
	SURVEY 2	99	0	545	455						
	DIFFERENCE		29	32	-61						

* Response Percentages are shown in tenths of a percent (NNN) and should be read as NN.N%.

37. Trying to get an understanding of minority groups, are
they spending:(1) Too much time; (2) About the right amount
of time; (3) Too little time; (0) Don't know.

	RESPONSES:	1	2	3	4	5	6	7	8	9
	NUMBER					NN.N%*				
CONTROL: BEAT 1										
SURVEY 1	108	74	491	435						
SURVEY 2	117	137	444	419						
DIFFERENCE		-63	47	16						
No FI: BEAT 2										
SURVEY 1	112	152	536	313						
SURVEY 2	150	107	527	367						
DIFFERENCE		45	9	-54						
SPECIAL FI: BEAT 3										
SURVEY 1	100	60	540	400						
SURVEY 2	84	83	417	500						
DIFFERENCE		-23	123	-100						

* Response Percentages are shown in tenths of a percent (NNN) and should be read as NN.N%.

38. Now I would like to know how fair you think the San Diego
Police are in dealing with various groups. Generally speaking, do you think the San Diego Police are: (1) Usually fair;
(2) Unfair to some people; (3) Usually unfair; (0) Don't know.

	RESPONSES:	1	2	3	4	5	6	7	8	9
	NUMBER					NN.N%*				
CONTROL: BEAT 1										
SURVEY 1	142	676	289	35						
SURVEY 2	155	716	239	45						
DIFFERENCE		-40	50	-10						
No FI: BEAT 2										
SURVEY 1	189	741	233	26						
SURVEY 2	208	788	154	58						
DIFFERENCE		-47	79	-32						
SPECIAL FI: BEAT 3										
SURVEY 1	153	647	294	59						
SURVEY 2	153	706	235	59						
DIFFERENCE		-59	59	0						

* Response Percentages are shown in tenths of a percent (NNN) and should be read as NN.N%.

39. When you say unfair to some people who did you have in mind?
    (DO NOT READ RESPONSES). (1) Whites; (2) Blacks; (3) Mexican-
    Americans; (4) Young whites; (5) Young blacks, Young Mexican-
    Americans, (6) Long haired men; (7) Rich people; (8) Poor
    people; (9) Other answers, specify:_____
    _____ ; (0) Refused to respond or can't specify.

	RESPONSES:	1	2	3	4	5	6	7	8	9
	NUMBER					NN.N%*				
CONTROL: BEAT 1										
SURVEY 1	24	42	83	167	0	83	167	0	125	333
SURVEY 2	34	59	206	0	0	353	29	0	29	324
DIFFERENCE		-17	-123	167	0	-270	138	0	96	9
No FI: BEAT 2										
SURVEY 1	26	115	192	77	77	0	192	0	38	308
SURVEY 2	23	43	87	87	43	261	261	0	43	174
DIFFERENCE		72	105	-10	34	-261	-69	0	-5	134
SPECIAL FI: BEAT 3										
SURVEY 1	32	94	94	94	63	31	219	0	63	344
SURVEY 2	32	0	219	63	63	156	94	0	0	406
DIFFERENCE		94	-125	31	0	-125	125	0	63	-62

* Response Percentages are shown in tenths of a percent (NNN) and should be read as NN.N%.

SAN DIEGO POLICE DEPARTMENT FI PROJECT - COMMUNITY ATTITUDINAL SURVEY RESULTS
RESPONSE PERCENTAGES BY BEAT

40. Some people say that police officers enjoy pushing people around
    and giving them a hard time. Other people don't think that this
    is true. What about the police in this neighborhood, do you think
    that most of them, (1) Never push people around? (2) Sometimes
    push people around? (3) Usually push people around? (4) Always
    push people around? (0) Don't know.

	RESPONSES:	1	2	3	4	5	6	7	8	9
	NUMBER					NN.N%*				
CONTROL: BEAT 1										
SURVEY 1	128	625	344	23	8					
SURVEY 2	142	768	197	21	14					
DIFFERENCE		-143	147	2	-6					
No FI: BEAT 2										
SURVEY 1	172	721	250	23	6					
SURVEY 2	185	578	389	22	11					
DIFFERENCE		143	-139	1	-5					
SPECIAL FI: BEAT 3										
SURVEY 1	142	592	380	28	0					
SURVEY 2	136	684	257	51	7					
DIFFERENCE		-92	123	-23	-7					

* Response Percentages are shown in tenths of a percent (NNN) and should be read as NN.N%.

41. People have different opinions as to what the police have the
right to do in stopping individual citizens outside their homes.
I would like to know whether you agree or disagree that the
police have the right to do certain things. To what extent do
you agree or disagree that the police have the right to stop you
if you appear suspicious to them and ask your name and address:
(1) Very much agree; (2) Somewhat agree; (3) Somewhat disagree;
(4) Very much disagree; (0) Don't know.

		RESPONSES: NUMBER	1	2	3	4	5 NN.N%*	6	7	8	9
CONTROL:	BEAT 1										
	SURVEY 1	159	692	164	50	94					
	SURVEY 2	178	713	169	62	56					
	DIFFERENCE		-21	-5	-12	38					
No FI:	BEAT 2										
	SURVEY 1	207	691	227	34	48					
	SURVEY 2	223	637	229	72	63					
	DIFFERENCE		54	-2	-38	-15					
SPECIAL FI:	BEAT 3										
	SURVEY 1	166	639	217	60	84					
	SURVEY 2	195	703	133	46	118					
	DIFFERENCE		-64	84	14	-34					

* Response Percentages are shown in tenths of a percent (NNN) and should be read as NN.N%.

42. To what extent do you agree or disagree that the police have the
right to stop you if you appear suspicious to them and ask you
what you are doing: (1) Very much agree; (2) Somewhat agree;
(3) Somewhat disagree; (4) Very much disagree; (0) Don't know.

		RESPONSES: NUMBER	1	2	3	4	5 NN.N%*	6	7	8	9
CONTROL:	BEAT 1										
	SURVEY 1	158	665	114	51	171					
	SURVEY 2	179	637	207	101	56					
	DIFFERENCE		28	-93	-50	115					
No FI:	BEAT 2										
	SURVEY 1	206	650	223	68	58					
	SURVEY 2	223	623	238	76	63					
	DIFFERENCE		27	-15	-8	-5					
SPECIAL FI:	BEAT 3										
	SURVEY 1	165	588	224	79	109					
	SURVEY 2	195	631	154	62	154					
	DIFFERENCE		-43	70	17	-45					

* Response Percentages are shown in tenths of a percent (NNN) and should be read as NN.N%.

43. To what extent do you agree or disagree that the police have the
    right to search you or your automobile if you appear suspicious
    to them without giving you a reason and without a search warrant:
    (1) Very much agree; (2) Somewhat agree; (3) Somewhat disagree;
    (4) Very much disagree; (0) Don't know.

		RESPONSES: NUMBER	1	2	3	4	5	6	7	8	9
						NN.N%*					
CONTROL:	BEAT 1										
	SURVEY 1	159	164	101	57	679					
	SURVEY 2	178	197	163	135	506					
	DIFFERENCE		-33	-62	-78	173					
No FI:	BEAT 2										
	SURVEY 1	207	150	169	164	517					
	SURVEY 2	222	122	167	203	509					
	DIFFERENCE		28	2	-39	8					
SPECIAL FI:	BEAT 3										
	SURVEY 1	163	98	129	117	656					
	SURVEY 2	193	181	67	83	668					
	DIFFERENCE		-83	62	34	-12					

* Response Percentages are shown in tenths of a percent (NNN) and should be read as NN.N%.

44. To what extent do you agree or disagree that the police have the
    right to search you or your automobile if you appear suspicious
    to them after giving you a reason, but without a search warrant:
    (1) Very much agree; (2) Somewhat agree; (3) Somewhat disagree;
    (4) Very much disagree; (0) Don't know.

		RESPONSES: NUMBER	1	2	3	4	5	6	7	8	9
						NN.N%*					
CONTROL:	BEAT 1										
	SURVEY 1	156	410	263	90	237					
	SURVEY 2	179	447	324	73	156					
	DIFFERENCE		-37	-61	17	81					
No FI:	BEAT 2										
	SURVEY 1	207	411	333	101	155					
	SURVEY 2	220	382	259	141	218					
	DIFFERENCE		29	74	-40	-63					
SPECIAL FI:	BEAT 3										
	SURVEY 1	164	323	360	104	213					
	SURVEY 2	195	354	287	82	277					
	DIFFERENCE		-31	73	22	-64					

* Response Percentages are shown in tenths of a percent (NNN) and should be read as NN.N%.

45. Did you ever see a police officer use physical force of some kind toward an individual? (1) Yes; (2) No.

		RESPONSES: NUMBER	1	2	3	4	5 NN.N%*	6	7	8	9
CONTROL:	BEAT 1										
	SURVEY 1	162	290	710							
	SURVEY 2	181	249	751							
	DIFFERENCE		41	-41							
No FI:	BEAT 2										
	SURVEY 1	208	269	731							
	SURVEY 2	224	348	652							
	DIFFERENCE		-79	79							
SPECIAL FI:	BEAT 3										
	SURVEY 1	171	363	637							
	SURVEY 2	202	356	644							
	DIFFERENCE		7	-7							

* Response Percentages are shown in tenths of a percent (NNN) and should be read as NN.N%.

46. Was that in this neighborhood? (1) Yes; (2) No.

		RESPONSES: NUMBER	1	2	3	4	5 NN.N%*	6	7	8	9
CONTROL:	BEAT 1										
	SURVEY 1	47	106	894							
	SURVEY 2	45	267	733							
	DIFFERENCE		-161	161							
No FI:	BEAT 2										
	SURVEY 1	56	268	732							
	SURVEY 2	78	205	795							
	DIFFERENCE		63	-63							
SPECIAL FI:	BEAT 3										
	SURVEY 1	62	290	710							
	SURVEY 2	71	197	803							
	DIFFERENCE		93	-93							

* Response Percentages are shown in tenths of a percent (NNN) and should be read as NN.N%.

47. Was it in the past 12 months? (1) Yes; (2) No.

	RESPONSES: NUMBER	1	2	3	4	5 NN.N%*	6	7	8	9
CONTROL: BEAT 1										
SURVEY 1	47	447	553							
SURVEY 2	45	444	556							
DIFFERENCE		3	-3							
No FI: BEAT 2										
SURVEY 1	56	571	429							
SURVEY 2	78	577	423							
DIFFERENCE		-6	6							
SPECIAL FI: BEAT 3										
SURVEY 1	62	597	403							
SURVEY 2	71	606	394							
DIFFERENCE		-9	9							

* Response Percentages are shown in tenths of a percent (NNN) and should be read as NN.N%.

48. Do you think the police officer was right or wrong to use force on the individual? (1) Right; (2) Wrong; (0) Don't know. Why?

	RESPONSES: NUMBER	1	2	3	4	5 NN.N%*	6	7	8	9
CONTROL: BEAT 1										
SURVEY 1	41	463	537							
SURVEY 2	41	390	610							
DIFFERENCE		73	-73							
No FI: BEAT 2										
SURVEY 1	53	547	453							
SURVEY 2	71	592	408							
DIFFERENCE		-45	45							
SPECIAL FI: BEAT 3										
SURVEY 1	58	397	603							
SURVEY 2	66	318	682							
DIFFERENCE		79	-79							

* Response Percentages are shown in tenths of a percent (NNN) and should be read as NN.N%.

49. Why do you think that people in this neighborhood don't provide more help to the police? (DO NOT READ ALTERNATIVES. IF MORE THAN ONE ANSWER GIVEN, PROBE FOR MOST IMPORTANT.) (1) People don't respect the police; (2) People don't want to get involved; (3) People are afraid of getting friends and neighbors mad at them; (4) People feel they can't do anything to help; (5) People are afraid of getting criminals against them; (6) People don't want to appear in court; (8) People don't know how to help or what to do; (9) Other answers, specify.

		RESPONSES: NUMBER	1	2	3	4	5 NN.N%*	6	7	8	9
CONTROL:	BEAT 1										
	SURVEY 1	73	192	479	27	14	14	0	0	137.	137
	SURVEY 2	104	115	269	10	48	48	10	0	48	452
	DIFFERENCE		77	210	17	-34	-34	-10	0	89	-315
No FI:	BEAT 2										
	SURVEY 1	106	151	396	94	47	19	0	0	66	226
	SURVEY 2	148	162	466	74	61	61	0	0	122	54
	DIFFERENCE		-11	-70	20	-14	-42	0	0	-56	172
SPECIAL FI:	BEAT 3										
	SURVEY 1	91	198	538	11	11	22	0	0	33	187
	SURVEY 2	121	198	388	33	25	50	8	0	0	298
	DIFFERENCE		0	150	-22	-14	-28	-8	0	33	-111

* Response Percentages are shown in tenths of a percent (NNN) and should be read as NN.N%.

50. I am going to ask some questions now about different kinds of crimes. In the past 12 months has anyone stolen anything from you or anyone who lives here--or criminally damaged property? (1) Yes; (2) No.

		RESPONSES: NUMBER	1	2	3	4	5 NN.N%*	6	7	8	9
CONTROL:	BEAT 1										
	SURVEY 1	162	259	741							
	SURVEY 2	181	309	691							
	DIFFERENCE		-50	50							
No FI:	BEAT 2										
	SURVEY 1	208	341	659							
	SURVEY 2	224	371	629							
	DIFFERENCE		-30	30							
SPECIAL FI:	BEAT 3										
	SURVEY 1	171	404	596							
	SURVEY 2	202	287	713							
	DIFFERENCE		117	-117							

* Response Percentages are shown in tenths of a percent (NNN) and should be read as NN.N%.

51. Did you see anything criminally damaged or something stolen or taken from anyone else in this neighborhood in the last 12 months? (1) Yes; (2) No.

		RESPONSES: NUMBER	1	2	3	4	5 NN.N%*	6	7	8	9
CONTROL:	BEAT 1										
	SURVEY 1	162	117	883							
	SURVEY 2	181	210	790							
	DIFFERENCE		-93	93							
No FI:	BEAT 2										
	SURVEY 1	208	178	822							
	SURVEY 2	224	402	598							
	DIFFERENCE		-224	224							
SPECIAL FI:	BEAT 3										
	SURVEY 1	171	158	842							
	SURVEY 2	202	213	787							
	DIFFERENCE		-55	55							

* Response Percentages are shown in tenths of a percent (NNN) and should be read as NN.N%.

52. In the last 12 months were you or anyone who lives here attacked in any way by another person, whether with fists or gun, knife, club, rock, or any other kind of weapon? Or, has anyone in your household been molested? (1) Yes; (2) No.

		RESPONSES: NUMBER	1	2	3	4	5 NN.N%*	6	7	8	9
CONTROL:	BEAT 1										
	SURVEY 1	162	31	969							
	SURVEY 2	181	33	967							
	DIFFERENCE		-2	2							
No FI:	BEAT 2										
	SURVEY 1	208	34	966							
	SURVEY 2	224	49	951							
	DIFFERENCE		-15	15							
SPECIAL FI:	BEAT 3										
	SURVEY 1	171	94	906							
	SURVEY 2	202	50	950							
	DIFFERENCE		44	-44							

* Response Percentages are shown in tenths of a percent (NNN) and should be read as NN.N%.

53. Did you see anyone in this neighborhood get attacked or molested in the last 12 months? (1) Yes; (2) No.

		RESPONSES: NUMBER	1	2	3	4	5 NN.N%*	6	7
CONTROL:	BEAT 1								
	SURVEY 1	162	6	994				
	SURVEY 2	181	28	972				
	DIFFERENCE		-22	22				
No FI:	BEAT 2								
	SURVEY 1	208	67	933				
	SURVEY 2	224	76	924				
	DIFFERENCE		-9	9				
SPECIAL FI:	BEAT 3								
	SURVEY 1	170	47	953				
	SURVEY 2	202	54	946				
	DIFFERENCE		-7	7				

* Response Percentages are shown in tenths of a percent (NNN) and should be read as NN.N%.

54. Of the crime incidents that you have observed in this neighborhood in the last 12 months, how many did you report to the police? (1) All; (2) Most; (3) Few; (4) None; (0) Don't know.

		RESPONSES: NUMBER	1	2	3	4	5 NN.N%*	6	7	8	9
CONTROL:	BEAT 1										
	SURVEY 1	38	342	26	79	553				
	SURVEY 2	78	397	90	26	487				
	DIFFERENCE		-55	-64	53	66				
No FI:	BEAT 2										
	SURVEY 1	83	373	96	84	446				
	SURVEY 2	135	637	67	44	252				
	DIFFERENCE		-264	29	40	194				
SPECIAL FI:	BEAT 3										
	SURVEY 1	75	453	53	27	467				
	SURVEY 2	180	538	50	38	375				
	DIFFERENCE		-85	3	-11	92				

* Response Percentages are shown in tenths of a percent (NNN) and should be read as NN.N%.

55. In general, why didn't you report all incidents? (DO NOT READ
    RESPONSES.) (1) Value of loss too small; (2) Police wouldn't
    help anyway; (3) Police make you feel dumb when you report to
    them; (4) Fear of reprisal from criminals; (5) Just didn't want
    to get involved; (6) Other

		RESPONSES: NUMBER	1	2	3	4	5 NN.N%*	6	7	8	9
CONTROL:	BEAT 1										
	SURVEY 1	27	481	148	0	37	37	296			
	SURVEY 2	45	244	200	22	22	22	489			
	DIFFERENCE		237	-52	-22	15	15	-193			
No FI:	BEAT 2										
	SURVEY 1	52	192	212	0	0	19	577			
	SURVEY 2	38	132	237	0	0	79	553			
	DIFFERENCE		60	-25	0	0	-60	24			
SPECIAL FI:	BEAT 3										
	SURVEY 1	47	149	340	21	0	43	447			
	SURVEY 2	32	156	250	31	31	94	438			
	DIFFERENCE		-7	90	-10	-31	-51	9			

* Response Percentages are shown in tenths of a percent (NNN) and should be read as NN.N%.

56. In the last 12 months how many times have you called the police
    about anyone or any problem in this neighborhood? (1) One;
    (2) Two; (3) Three; (4) Four; (5) Five; (6) Six; (7) Seven;
    (8) Eight; (9) Nine or more; (0) None.

		RESPONSES: NUMBER	1	2	3	4	5 NN.N%*	6	7	8	9	0
CONTROL:	BEAT 1											
	SURVEY 1	162	667	185	80	49	12	0	6	0	0	0
	SURVEY 2	181	724	149	72	22	11	6	6	6	0	6
	DIFFERENCE		-57	36	8	27	1	-6	0	-6	0	-6
No FI:	BEAT 2											
	SURVEY 1	208	625	183	125	38	10	5	10	0	0	5
	SURVEY 2	224	603	143	112	36	27	22	13	0	18	27
	DIFFERENCE		22	40	13	2	-17	-17	-3	0	-18	-22
SPECIAL FI:	BEAT 3											
	SURVEY 1	171	591	228	105	23	0	18	18	0	0	18
	SURVEY 2	202	599	193	104	50	20	10	10	5	0	10
	DIFFERENCE		-8	35	1	-27	-20	8	8	-5	0	8

* Response Percentages are shown in tenths of a percent (NNN) and should be read as NN.N%.

> 57. What was the last call to the police about? (1) Property stolen;
> (2) Juvenile disturbances (NOT drug related); (3) Adult fighting
> --family quarrel-disturbing the peace; (4) Damaging public or
> private property--tampering with an automobile; (5) Burglary--
> attempting to enter a residence or business; (6) Suspicious
> people in car--prowlers or trespassers; (7) Dog nuisance;
> (8) Accident or illness; (9) Other answers--specify.

		RESPONSES: NUMBER	1	2	3	4	5 NN.N%*	6	7	8	9
CONTROL:	BEAT 1										
	SURVEY 1	52	115	115	250	115	96	96	38	77	96
	SURVEY 2	50	280	60	120	120	80	40	100	80	120
	DIFFERENCE		-165	55	130	-5	16	56	-62	-3	-24
No FI:	BEAT 2										
	SURVEY 1	78	244	192	128	51	103	13	13	167	90
	SURVEY 2	85	106	153	59	212	188	47	35	106	94
	DIFFERENCE		138	39	69	-161	-85	-34	-22	61	-4
SPECIAL FI:	BEAT 3										
	SURVEY 1	70	143	171	143	114	114	0	57	100	157
	SURVEY 2	77	273	156	221	52	39	65	0	91	104
	DIFFERENCE		-130	15	-78	62	75	-65	57	9	53

* Response Percentages are shown in tenths of a percent (NNN) and should be read as NN.N%.

SAN DIEGO POLICE DEPARTMENT FI PROJECT - COMMUNITY ATTITUDINAL SURVEY RESULTS
RESPONSE PERCENTAGES BY BEAT

> 58. Were you satisfied about the length of time it took the police
> to get here? (1) Very satisfied; (2) Slightly satisfied;
> (3) Slight dissatisfied; (4) Very dissatisfied; (0) Don't know.

		RESPONSES: NUMBER	1	2	3	4 NN.N%*	5	6	7	8	9
CONTROL:	BEAT 1										
	SURVEY 1	51	588	98	59	255					
	SURVEY 2	44	318	68	136	477					
	DIFFERENCE		270	30	-77	-222					
No FI:	BEAT 2										
	SURVEY 1	75	453	120	93	333					
	SURVEY 2	82	268	85	122	524					
	DIFFERENCE		185	35	-29	-191					
SPECIAL FI:	BEAT 3										
	SURVEY 1	61	443	98	66	393					
	SURVEY 2	74	432	41	108	419					
	DIFFERENCE		11	57	-42	-26					

* Response Percentages are shown in tenths of a percent (NNN) and should be read as NN.N%.

> 59. Overall, were you satisfied with the way the police handled the
> situation? (1) Very satisfied; (2) Slightly satisfied;
> (3) Slight dissatisfied; (4) Very dissatisfied; (0) Don't know.

		RESPONSES: NUMBER	1	2	3	4	5	6	7	8	9
						NN.N%*					
CONTROL:	BEAT 1										
	SURVEY 1	52	673	38	77	212					
	SURVEY 2	48	396	104	21	479					
	DIFFERENCE		277	-66	56	-267					
No FI:	BEAT 2										
	SURVEY 1	78	538	141	64	256					
	SURVEY 2	87	368	92	103	437					
	DIFFERENCE		170	49	-39	-181					
SPECIAL FI:	BEAT 3										
	SURVEY 1	63	444	143	111	302					
	SURVEY 2	72	569	97	28	306					
	DIFFERENCE		-125	46	83	-4					

* Response Percentages are shown in tenths of a percent (NNN) and should be read as NN.N%

> 60. The next few questions concern any tickets, arrests, and other
> police contacts you may have made. The reason for these
> questions is not to pry into your personal life, but to find
> out how much chance you've had to see how police behave. Have
> you received a traffic ticket in the last 12 months? (1) Yes;
> (2) No.

		RESPONSES: NUMBER	1	2	3	4	5	6	7	8	9
						NN.N%*					
CONTROL	BEAT 1										
	SURVEY 1	161	168	832							
	SURVEY 2	181	204	796							
	DIFFERENCE		-36	36							
No FI:	BEAT 2										
	SURVEY 1	207	237	763							
	SURVEY 2	223	126	874							
	DIFFERENCE		111	-111							
SPECIAL FI:	BEAT 3										
	SURVEY 1	171	222	778							
	SURVEY 2	199	186	814							
	DIFFERENCE		36	-36							

* Response Percentages are shown in tenths of a percent (NNN) and should be read as NN.N%.

61. Was there anything about the way the police officer acted that
    you liked? (1) Yes; (2) No. If yes, what.

	RESPONSES:	1	2	3	4	5	6	7	8	9
	NUMBER					NN.N%*				
CONTROL: BEAT 1										
SURVEY 1	27	519	481							
SURVEY 2	37	541	459							
DIFFERENCE		-22	22							
No FI: BEAT 2										
SURVEY 1	48	646	354							
SURVEY 2	28	679	321							
DIFFERENCE		-33	33							
SPECIAL FI: BEAT 3										
SURVEY 1	38	605	395							
SURVEY 2	37	297	703							
DIFFERENCE		308	-308							

* Response Percentages are shown in tenths of a percent (NNN) and should be read as NN.N%.

62. Was there anything about the way the officer acted that you
    didn't like? (1) Yes; (2) No; If yes, what.

	RESPONSES:	1	2	3	4	5	6	7	8	9
	NUMBER					NN.N%*				
CONTROL: BEAT 1										
SURVEY 1	27	259	741							
SURVEY 2	37	324	676							
DIFFERENCE		-65	65							
No FI: BEAT 2										
SURVEY 1	49	347	653							
SURVEY 2	28	357	643							
DIFFERENCE		-10	10							
SPECIAL FI: BEAT 3										
SURVEY 1	38	237	763							
SURVEY 2	37	405	595							
DIFFERENCE		-168	168							

* Response Percentages are shown in tenths of a percent (NNN) and should be read as NN.N%.

> 63. In this neighborhood, have you been stopped and questioned or
>   searched by the police in the last 12 months for anything other
>   than a traffic violation? (1) Yes; (2) No.

		RESPONSES: NUMBER	1	2	3	4	5 NN.N%*	6	7	8	9
CONTROL:	BEAT 1										
	SURVEY 1	162	80	920							
	SURVEY 2	181	44	956							
	DIFFERENCE		36	-36							
No FI:	BEAT 2										
	SURVEY 1	208	63	938							
	SURVEY 2	222	59	941							
	DIFFERENCE		4	-3							
SPECIAL FI:	BEAT 3										
	SURVEY 1	171	94	906							
	SURVEY 2	199	151	849							
	DIFFERENCE		-57	57							

* Response Percentages are shown in tenths of a percent (NNN) and should be read as NN.N%.

> 64. Was there anything about the way the officer acted that you liked?
>   (1) Yes; (2) No.

		RESPONSES: NUMBER	1	2	3	4	5 NN.N%*	6	7	8	9
CONTROL:	BEAT 1										
	SURVEY 1	13	462	538							
	SURVEY 2	7	714	286							
	DIFFERENCE		-252	252							
No FI:	BEAT 2										
	SURVEY 1	13	462	538							
	SURVEY 2	13	385	615							
	DIFFERENCE		77	-77							
SPECIAL FI:	BEAT 3										
	SURVEY 1	16	375	625							
	SURVEY 2	30	467	533							
	DIFFERENCE		-92	92							

* Response Percentages are shown in tenths of a percent (NNN) and should be read as NN.N%.

> 65. Was there anything about the way the police officer acted that you didn't like? (1) Yes; (2) No.

		RESPONSES: NUMBER	1	2	3	4	5	6	7	8	9
							NN.N%*				
CONTROL:	BEAT 1										
	SURVEY 1	13	538	462							
	SURVEY 2	7	143	857							
	DIFFERENCE		395	-395							
No FI:	BEAT 2										
	SURVEY 1	13	385	615							
	SURVEY 2	13	385	615							
	DIFFERENCE		0	0							
SPECIAL FI:	BEAT 3										
	SURVEY 1	16	500	500							
	SURVEY 2	30	467	533							
	DIFFERENCE		33	-33							

* Response Percentages are shown in tenths of a percent (NNN) and should be read as NN.N%.

> 66. In this neighborhood within the last 12 months, have you seen the police stop and question or search anyone? (1) Yes; (2) No.

		RESPONSES: NUMBER	1	2	3	4	5	6	7	8	9
							NN.N%*				
CONTROL:	BEAT 1										
	SURVEY 1	158	449	551							
	SURVEY 2	181	387	613							
	DIFFERENCE		62	-62							
No FI:	BEAT 2										
	SURVEY 1	208	385	615							
	SURVEY 2	220	327	673							
	DIFFERENCE		58	-58							
SPECIAL FI:	BEAT 3										
	SURVEY 1	171	380	620							
	SURVEY 2	201	343	657							
	DIFFERENCE		37	-37							

* Response Percentages are shown in tenths of a percent (NNN) and should be read as NN.N%.

67. Was there anything about the way the officer acted that you did
    like? (1) Yes; (2) No.

		RESPONSES: NUMBER	1	2	3	4	5 NN.N%	6	7	8	9
CONTROL:	BEAT 1										
	SURVEY 1	71	437	563							
	SURVEY 2	69	246	754							
	DIFFERENCE		191	-191							
No FI:	BEAT 2										
	SURVEY 1	79	380	620							
	SURVEY 2	72	333	667							
	DIFFERENCE		47	-47							
SPECIAL FI:	BEAT 3										
	SURVEY 1	60	383	617							
	SURVEY 2	69	290	710							
	DIFFERENCE		93	-93							

* Response Percentages are shown in tenths of a percent (NNN) and should be read as NN.N%.

68. Was there anything about the way the police officer acted that
    you didn't like? (1) Yes; (2) No.

		RESPONSES: NUMBER	1	2	3	4	5 NN.N%	6	7	8	9
CONTROL:	BEAT 1										
	SURVEY 1	71	141	859							
	SURVEY 2	69	72	928							
	DIFFERENCE		69	-69							
No FI:	BEAT 2										
	SURVEY 1	80	113	888							
	SURVEY 2	72	97	903							
	DIFFERENCE		16	-15							
SPECIAL FI:	BEAT 3										
	SURVEY 1	62	145	855							
	SURVEY 2	69	116	884							
	DIFFERENCE		29	-29							

* Response Percentages are shown in tenths of a percent (NNN) and should be read as NN.N%.

E. COMMENTS ON OPEN-ENDED SURVEY QUESTIONS

Seventeen of the questions in the Community Attitude Survey permitted "write-in"
responses in addition to the more structured multiple choice options. For
analysis purposes, it was originally intended to aggregate these responses by
survey, beat, and age group. Preliminary analysis indicated that the number
of write-in responses was not sufficiently large to provide meaningful comparisons, particularly between beats and age groups. For example, consider
Question 21, "In the last 12 months have you noticed any change in the way
police operate in this neighborhood?" This question was specifically included in the survey to elicit the extent, if any, to which citizens perceived
changes in patrol operations. Responses to this question from both surveys
in each of the beats are presented in Table B-7.

The survey results provide a single conclusion, that citizens perceived an
increase in patrol activity. Meaningful differences between beats and age
groups were not substantiated, nor was there a significant change between
surveys. These findings were typical of those for other open-ended questions,
which in most instances had even fewer numbers of responses, and for this
reason permitted meaningful conclusions only in an aggregate sense. Therefore, the findings for the open-ended questions presented in Table B-8 are
limited to summary-type information for those specific questions where
sufficient responses were elicited to provide meaningful comments.

Table B-7. Summary of Write-In Responses to Question #21

BEAT	RESPONSE	SURVEY NUMBER	AGE GROUP				TOTAL
			16-19	20-34	35-49	50+	
C O N T R O L	More Frequent Patrols	1	2	7	7	5	21
		2	0	2	5	11	18
	Less Frequent Patrols	1	1	1	0	0	2
		2	0	0	0	0	0
	Faster Response Time	1	0	1	0	4	5
		2	0	0	0	0	0
	More Courteous	1	0	0	1	1	2
		2	0	0	1	0	1
	Other	1	0	0	2	1	3
		2	0	1	1	0	2
	Total	1	3	9	10	11	33
		2	0	3	7	11	21
N O F I	More Frequent Patrols	1	0	8	5	2	15
		2	5	14	9	4	32
	Less Frequent Patrols	1	0	2	3	1	6
		2	1	1	0	1	3
	Faster Response Time	1	2	0	0	0	2
		2	0	0	0	0	0
	More Courteous	1	0	0	0	0	0
		2	0	1	0	1	2
	Other	1	1	2	0	0	3
		2	0	0	2	0	2
	Total	1	3	12	8	3	26
		2	6	16	11	6	39
S P E C I A L F I	More Frequent Patrols	1	2	17	3	3	25
		2	2	6	9	3	20
	Less Frequent Patrols	1	2	3	2	1	8
		2	1	0	0	0	1
	Faster Response Time	1	0	1	0	0	1
		2	0	0	0	0	0
	More Courteous	1	1	1	4	1	7
		2	0	0	1	0	1
	Other	1	2	4	1	0	7
		2	0	0	3	0	3
	Total	1	7	26	10	5	48
		2	3	6	13	3	25

Table B-8. Summary of Responses to Open-Ended Questions (Sheet 1 of 3)

QUESTION	SURVEY NUMBER	TOTAL NUMBER OF RESPONSES	TOTAL NUMBER OF WRITE-IN RESPONSES	COMMENTS
12. What types of people do you think commit most crimes in this neighborhood?	1	348	40	The largest category (16) was unemployed, the second largest (6) was young people.
	2	376	52	The largest category (11) was low income people.
19. In this neighborhood is there anything in particular about police services that you like?	1	539	0	No responses.
	2	606	33	The largest category (12) was helicopter patrol.
20. In this neighborhood is there anything in particular about police services that you don't like?	1	541	15	No specific pattern of responses
	2	606	24	Answers were not concentrated in any area; the range of answers covered 17 different responses.
21. In the past 12 months have you noticed any changes in the way the police operate in this neighborhood? If yes, what?	1	499	118	62 reported more patrol activity.
	2	553	88	58 reported more patrol activity.
39. When you say unfair to some people, whom do you have in mind?	1	82	27	Minorities and youths received most frequent mention.
	2	89	38	11 cited youths, and 11 cited minorities in general.
48. Do you think the police officer was right or wrong to use force on the individual? Why?	1	152	126	51 indicated force was necessary.
	2	178	180	72 said force was not necessary, and 33 said too much force was used.

(Continued)

Table B-8. Summary of Responses to Open-Ended Questions (Sheet 2 of 3)

QUESTION	SURVEY NUMBER	TOTAL NUMBER OF RESPONSES	TOTAL NUMBER OF WRITE-IN RESPONSES	COMMENTS
49. Why do you think that people in this neighborhood don't provide help to the police?	1	270	51	Most respondents indicated that people do provide help, but that some citizens don't trust or are afraid of the police.
	2	373	90	49 said that people do provide help and 13 said that there are no problems in the neighborhood.
55. In general why didn't you report all incidents?	1	126	59	Majority indicated that others reported incidents.
	2	115	38	32 stated that someone else reported the incident.
57. What was the last call to the police about?	1	200	23	No discernible pattern in either survey. Many different responses.
	2	212	21	
61. Was there anything about the way the police officer acted that you liked? (Traffic ticket). If yes, what?	1	113	68	Number of responses too small to provide meaningful findings.
	2	102	50	Polite and courteous; and easy going or nice manners were mentioned most frequently.
62. Was there anything about the way the police officer acted that you didn't like? (Traffic ticket). If yes, what?	1	114	33	Number of responses too small to provide meaningful findings. Most said rude manner, attitude or remarks; some said unfair.
	2	102	37	
64. Was there anything about the way the officer acted that you liked? (Not traffic). If yes, what?	1	42	18	Number of responses too small to provide meaningful findings. Most respondents said polite, friendly or nice.
	2	50	24	

Table B-8. Summary of Responses to Open-Ended Questions (Sheet 3 of 3)

QUESTIONS	SURVEY NUMBER	TOTAL NUMBER OF RESPONSES	TOTAL NUMBER OF WRITE-IN RESPONSES	COMMENTS
65. Was there anything about the way the police officer acted that you didn't like? (Not traffic). If yes, what?	1	42	20	Number of responses too small to provide meaningful findings. Most said there was no reason for stop or search. Some said intimidation or threat of force.
	2	50	20	
67. If you observed police stop or search anyone, was there anything that you did like?	1	210	84	Number of responses too small to provide meaningful conclusions. Most respondents mentioned polite, courteous, friendly; some said business-like or handled situation well.
	2	210	61	
68. If you observed police stop or search anyone, was there anything that you did not like?	1	213	28	Number of responses too small to provide meaningful conclusions. Most respondents said police were rude or intimidated victims.
	2	210	28	
Last Question. Is there anything else that you'd like to mention about the problem of crime in this neighborhood or about the SDPD?	1	84	84	Extremely varied pattern of responses in both surveys. More frequent responses were as follows: Police are doing a good job; need more policemen; need more patrol; need better communication between police and juveniles; need improved relations between police and community; need more authority for police, in particular vis-a-vis the courts; police should be college educated or take more social sciences courses; police should respond more rapidly.
	2	86	86	

APPENDIX C: Sample SDC Observers' Log and FI Observation Forms Plus Copies of Actual FI Reports

(Subject names and addresses have been removed)

OBSERVER: _Streech_   DATE: _February 26, 1974_

STUDY AREA: _Control_   SHIFT: _P-2_

OFFICER(S): ~~Peterson~~ & ~~Anderson~~

TIMES	EVENT
1505 - 1510	Illegal street crossing by long-haired pedestrian in downtown area. Cited.
1520 - 1525	Traffic Stop: Faulty brake light, mexican driver. Cited.
1525 - 1540	Responded to house call. Took women to emergency room in hospital.
1540 - 1610	Responded to man down call. Took unconscious male to emergency room in hospital.
1627 - 1635	Traffic stop: smoking car - two blocks. Ran wanted auto and person checks F I'd; no search; an adult + juvenile. F.I.# 34,188 - ~~Peterson~~ Keith — Juvenile F.I.# 34,189 - ~~Peterson~~, adult.
1640 - 1705	Out of service at city communications shop. (Dispatcher had complained about unit's radio transmissions.)
1725 - 1728	Stopped 13 year old boy and warned him about jaywalking.
1730 - 1735	Traffic stop - illegal left turn. Cited.
1737 - 1748	Stopped black pedestrian "didn't look right." Questioned at length. Did not F.I. as he was local. A known ex-con.
1805 - 1810	Observed elderly wino drunk on sidewalk. Called for a cage car, who transported him to jail.
1820 - 1825	Rechecked report on above drunk.

OBSERVER _STREICH_   DATE _2/26/74_   BEAT _11_

SHIFT (P1) (P2) (P3) _Two-men_   NUMBER OF MEN _Patrol/Ambulance_ TYPE UNIT

===

Reason for Stop: _Smoking car, cited. Officers "didn't like the looks of driver and passenger."_

Time _1617-37_   Stress _no_
Weather _clear_   Number _34, 188_
Light _Daylight - late afternoon sunshine_

APPROACH: Verbal _Courteous_
     Hands/Arms _at sides_
     Trunk/Head _normal, not aggressive_
     Intrusion:Space _non-intrusive_   Visual _close scrutiny_

SUBJECT: Appearance _Casual clothes, not slovenly looking, black juvenile_

     Attitude _Answered questions only, but not belligerent_

BYSTANDER(S): Appearance _none present_

     Attitude

(Use reverse if needed)

Reason for Stop: _Same as above_

Time _1617-37_   Stress _no_
Weather _Clear_   Number _34, 189_
Light _Daylight - late afternoon sunshine_

APPROACH: Verbal _Firm questioning; demanding but not abrasive_
     Hands/Arms _at sides_
     Trunk/Head _normal, not aggressive_
     Intrusion:Space _non-intrusive_   Visual _Very close scrutiny_

SUBJECT: Appearance _Casual dress_

     Attitude _Evasive, but not belligerent_

BYSTANDER(S): Appearance _none present_

     Attitude

(Use reverse if needed)

C-2

FI Report #34189

NAME (L): ▓▓▓▓ (F) DAVEY BRUCE (MI) — DATE 2-26-71 — TIME 1620 — BEAT B — # OFFICERS TWO — REFER TO: ROBBERY

SEX: (M) F — RACE: WHT (BLK) MEX AM — OTHER: — DOB 8-17-55 — AGE 18 — HEIGHT 600 — WEIGHT 170 — SELEC. SERV./SOC. SEC. #

HAIR: BLK — EYES: BLU — ADDRESS: ▓▓▓▓ — CITY S.D. — STATE

VEHICLE LIC. NO.: ▓▓ — STATE CAL — VEH. YR. 66 — MAKE CHEV — MODEL 2DR — COLOR TOP WHT BOTTOM — ( ) DRIVER ( ) PASSENGER

DRIVER'S LIC. NO. N3159760 — STATE CAL — REG. OWNER - ADDRESS SAME

INTERIOR — COLOR UPHOLSTERY: BLK
(✓) CUSTOM ( ) RIPPED
( ) STANDARD
( ) BENCH SEAT (✓) BUCKET

ACCESSORIES:
( ) STEREO TAPE
(✓) EQUIP ADDED
( ) EQUIP MISSING
( ) UNIQUE ITEM

DAMAGE:
( ) L. SIDE
( ) R. SIDE
(✓) FRONT
( ) REAR

EXTERIOR:
(✓) LEVEL ALTERED
(✓) RUST/PRIMER
( ) VINYL TOP
( ) DECORATIVE PAINT
( ) PLAQUE
( ) DECAL
( ) CUSTOM WHEELS
( ) TINT/COVERED WINDOWS

SEX M — RACE N — NAME (LAST) ▓▓▓▓ — (FIRST) KEITH ALFRED — ADDRESS ▓▓▓ SD — BIRTH DATE 11-22-5?

Subject descriptors (circled):
HAIR STYLE: B (N) L C P R T
MARKS/SCARS: T S B A H (C)
EYES: (G) P C M
BUILD: H (M) T
HEIGHT: (T) A S
AGE: O (M) J
PECULIARITIES: B M F L C S (N)
GENERAL APPEAR.: U S D (C) M T
COMPLEXION: L (M) D A F

CLOTHING grid (circled): HAT 03, SHIRT 29, PANTS 39

LOCATION OF CONTACT: 600 S. 30TH — NICKNAME:
(A) CIRCUMSTANCES FOR STOP: TRAFFIC STOP
(B) CRIME POTENTIAL: 459-211-496.1 — FI# 34189
(C) WAS INQUIRY MADE? — MARSHAL (YES) NO — SHERIFF (YES) NO — DMV YES NO — NCIC YES NO — PERSON SEARCH YES (NO) — VEH. SEARCH YES (NO)

—REMARKS—
VEH. HAS NUMEROUS STREAKS OF PRIMER ALL AROUND. INTERIOR BLK ROLL & TUCK W/ BUCKETS. ▓▓▓ WEARING TAN VINYL HAT BACKWARD - THICK, WIRE FRAMED GLASSES

KEY PUNCH/FI PROJECT — APPROVED BY — OFFICER M.D. STANLEY — BADGE 975 — WATCH 2

FI Report #34188

NAME (L): ▓▓▓ KEITH ALFRED (F) (MI) — DATE 2-26-71 — TIME 1630 — BEAT 18 — # OFFICERS PRESENT 2 — REFER TO: ROBBERY

SEX: (M) F — RACE: WHT (BLK) MEX AM — OTHER: — DOB 11-22-5? — AGE 16 — HEIGHT BLK — WEIGHT BRN — SELEC. SERV./SOC. SEC. #

HAIR: BLK — EYES: BRN — ADDRESS 216 S. 33 — CITY S.D. — STATE CA

VEHICLE LIC. NO.: ▓▓ — STATE CALIF — VEH. YR. 66 — MAKE CHEV — MODEL 2DR — COLOR TOP WHITE BOTTOM — ( ) DRIVER (✓) PASSENGER

DRIVER'S LIC. NO. NONE — STATE — REG. OWNER - ADDRESS ▓▓▓

INTERIOR — COLOR UPHOLSTERY:
(✓) CUSTOM ( ) RIPPED
( ) STANDARD
( ) BENCH SEAT (✓) BUCKET

ACCESSORIES:
( ) STEREO TAPE
(✓) EQUIP ADDED
( ) EQUIP MISSING
( ) UNIQUE ITEM

DAMAGE:
( ) L. SIDE
( ) R. SIDE
(✓) FRONT
(✓) REAR

EXTERIOR:
(✓) LEVEL ALTERED
(✓) RUST/PRIMER
( ) VINYL TOP
( ) DECORATIVE PAINT
(✓) PLAQUE
(✓) DECAL
(✓) CUSTOM WHEELS
( ) TINT/COVERED WINDOWS

SEX M — RACE N — NAME (LAST) ▓▓▓ — (FIRST) DAVEY BRUCE — ADDRESS ▓▓▓ — BIRTH DATE 8-17-55

Subject descriptors (circled):
HAIR STYLE: B (N) L C P R T
MARKS/SCARS: T S B A H (N)
EYES: G P C M (N)
BUILD: H M (T)
HEIGHT: T (A) S
AGE: O M (Y) J
PECULIARITIES: (B) M F L C (S) N
GENERAL APPEAR.: U S D (C) M T
COMPLEXION: L (M) D A F

CLOTHING grid (circled): HAT 10, SHIRT 25, PANTS 37 40, SHOES 89

LOCATION OF CONTACT: 30TH & VALLEY — NICKNAME:
(A) CIRCUMSTANCES FOR STOP: TRAFFIC
(B) CRIME POTENTIAL: 459-211-496.1 — FI# 34188
(C) WAS INQUIRY MADE? — MARSHAL (YES) NO — SHERIFF (YES) NO — DMV YES NO — NCIC YES NO — PERSON SEARCH YES (NO) — VEH. SEARCH YES (NO)

—REMARKS—
NO ID - VERY DEFENSIVE. VERY SPARSE MUSTACHE. APPEARED TO HAVE FRECKLES.

KEY PUNCH/FI PROJECT — APPROVED BY — OFFICER J.F. CONNOLLY 425 — BADGE 425 — WATCH 2-1

North East Multi-Regional
Training, Inc.
1 Smoke Tree Plaza, Suite 111
North Aurora, IL 60542

C-3